G000254304

ULTIMA
Muay Thai

Bob Spour

ULTIMATE
Muay Thai

Bob Spour

CROWOOD

First published in 2004 by
The Crowood Press Ltd
Ramsbury, Marlborough
Wiltshire SN8 2HR

www.crowood.com

© Bob Spour 2004

All rights reserved. No part of this publication may be reproduced or
transmitted in any form or by any means, electronic or mechanical,
including photocopy, recording, or any information storage and retrieval
system, without permission in writing from the publishers.

British Library Cataloguing-in-Publication Data
A catalogue record for this book is available from the British Library.

ISBN 1 86126 671 5

Disclaimer
Please note that the author and the publisher of this book are not
responsible in any manner whatsoever for any damage, or injury of any
kind, that may result from practising, or applying, the techniques
and/or following the instructions described in this publication. Since
the physical activities described in this book may be too strenuous in
nature for some readers to engage in safely, it is essential that a doctor
be consulted prior to undertaking training.

Typeset by Jean Cussons Typesetting, Diss, Norfolk

Printed and bound in Great Britain by Biddles Ltd, King's Lynn

Contents

Foreword

I have known Bob Spour for more years than I care to remember, although once down on paper, that seems a bit harsh. What I mean is, when I see Bob, he reminds me just how many years we've been in this business! As the Editor of three martial arts publications, namely: *Combat Magazine*, *Traditional Karate Magazine* and *Taekwondo and Korean Martial Arts Magazine*, I have the good fortune to meet, mix and mingle with some of the biggest names in World martial arts. Amongst the most senior names in the World of Muay Thai is right where I'd place Bob. Having interviewed Bob, watched him teach in class and at seminars and having featured many articles that he wrote for use within *Combat*, I can honestly say that there are very few people who are as learned on the subject of Muay Thai, as he. He seems to have an instinctive feel for his chosen and much loved art of Muay Thai. A very open and candid person by nature, Bob knows exactly how to make his point and thereby impart his knowledge to any willing or interested party. Always keen to show you the correct way to do things, an hour can fly by when he 'gets into his stride'!

Humility, courtesy, respect and etiquette are all his watchwords, which is why he can interact with anyone. Allowing him into your club could be regarded as looking at your martial art of choice through a different set of eyes, as he can make you appreciate what you have, to a greater level. In short, whether you're bored or fascinated, mildly interested or fanatical, Bob has something to teach you.

My reasons for writing this preface in the fashion I have are simple – this book has something to offer you regardless of your level of experience or interest! If it only offers the reader 5 per cent of the enthusiasm that Bob has for the subject of Muay Thai, it should end up on the bestsellers list, very soon!

I'm sure you'll enjoy it as well as learn a great deal about Muay Thai and yourself.

Sawadee Krap!

Paul S. Clifton
Editor

Combat Magazine
Traditional Karate Magazine
Taekwondo and Korean Martial Arts Magazine

Preface

The author has trained in the martial arts for over thirty-five years and has been teaching for at least twenty-five years of that time. He is a qualified Black belt in two styles of Karate (Goju-ryu and Shoto-kan), a 3rd Dan Black belt in Full Contact Karate, a 4th Dan Black belt in Kick-boxing, a qualified practitioner of Escrima, an experienced boxing coach, Senior Instructor to the British Combat Association, Regional Head of the Technical Committee of the British Thai Boxing Council, a qualified Judge and Referee (qualifying in Thailand), Chief Instructor of the Phraya Pichai Muay Thai Camps International and an ex-member of the Special Forces. Bob was also a regular columnist for *Traditional Karate Magazine* and *Combat Magazine* and has also written for the magazine *Martial Arts Illustrated*. Bob is the Course Director to Mindworks Technologies, an organization devoted to improving communication skills, enhancing performance in individuals and groups, motivational training seminars and life coaching. He qualified as an NLP practitioner and Trainer under Dr Richard Bandler and also holds a BA (Hons) degree in Drama and Theatre Arts.

Fig. 1   The Author, Bob Spour.

Introduction

Muay Thai, or Thai Boxing as it is commonly known, is a martial art prone to misinterpretation. In the UK alone there are at least ten associations, some of which teach a mixture of techniques culled from Full Contact Karate, Boxing, Taekwondo, Kickboxing, Savate and even Kung Fu! It is difficult, if not impossible therefore, for the novice to know whether the art they are practising is any one of these or the art of real Muay Thai itself. This book wishes to redress the balance by giving the reader an appreciation of the way Muay Thai is taught in Thailand – the ancestral home of the art.

The author has thirty-seven years' experience of the martial arts and twenty of those years were spent studying Muay Thai. He currently runs a worldwide group under the auspices of the Thai Boxing International Board of Control with over forty clubs internationally. He has written for various magazines over a ten-year period on Muay Thai and is considered one of the leading teachers in the art worldwide.

The techniques demonstrated herein, reflect those currently being used in Thailand. It is these techniques that win the matches you can see every week in the main stadiums of Bangkok and the provinces. It is these techniques, that, for the first time, have been put into print in a coherent form working up from Day 1 of training over a three-month period. It forms therefore the essentials of Muay Thai.

A book can never replace a good teacher and the author has gone to great pains to explain how each technique should be practised. This book would also, therefore, serve as a useful source manual to any teacher of Muay Thai. But be aware that Muay Thai is constantly evolving. In the ring, the tools you have must work! If they don't do the job, then they will adapt to suit the fight. This is what makes it one of the most practical fighting arts in the world today. The journey that is Muay Thai is a long and interesting one. Let this book be your first step.

1 History and Rituals: the Roots of Muay Thai

History

Thailand has been prolific in producing some of the best empty-hand fighters in the world. Their training methods produce well-conditioned and physically fit fighters who are offensive in approach rather than defensive. Their attitude of no surrender in the ring is a legacy from their past, an attitude shaped by a history chequered by attacks on their culture, towns and cities.

To place Muay Thai into a historical perspective is a difficult task as Thailand's historical records are, alas, incomplete. The earliest records were lost in 1767 when Burma laid siege to Thailand's ancient capital Ayuddhaya. The city was eventually ransacked and put to the torch so all treasures, books, records, works of art and the royal archives were destroyed. All that remains are the fragments of a society pieced together by anthropologists from information taken from Burmese, Cambodian, Chinese and early European writings. In this chapter I wish to take a brief look at the history of Muay Thai. As stated above, actual records are incomplete but stories and anecdotes exist that illustrate the way in which the fighting arts of Thailand have developed.

It is this type of environment that shaped the Thai, their culture, their beliefs and of course gave them their attributes of fierce independence. For centuries they waged wars internally and against neighbouring states until the rise of the powerful and popular rebel Phraya Taksin. It was Taksin who liberated Ayuddhaya and, with the help of Phraya Pichai took overall control of the other Thai principalities. A relative period of peace ensued and Thailand as the nation we now know started to develop. It is not possible, however, in a book of this nature to go into the intricacies of Thai history, culture and myth. The remit of this chapter is to give basic information to help the reader understand the background to the development of Muay Thai.

As we have seen, the Thai have always been a fiercely independent nation having never been subjected to colonization by a foreign power (unlike their close neighbours). The popular culture of Muay Thai is liberally sprinkled with stories of their heroes and heroines – individuals who were responsible for the country's development and, ultimately, its economic growth.

One of the earliest records of a hand-to-hand confrontation comes from The Chiang Mai Annals. They relate a story of King Sen Muang Ma (1411) whose two sons Yi Kumkam and Fang Ken fought for the throne and after a lengthy battle neither could beat the other's army and so it was suggested by Fang Ken that they fight man to man in single combat. Each side selected a champion fighter from among their army of supporters who would fight till the first blood was drawn. Evidently the fight lasted several hours until Yi Kumkam's champion won and Kumkam became the new King.

Resolving disputes by this method was not uncommon in Thailand (even the Europeans used this method) and a very famous incident like this took place during the reign of Taksin (1767–82).

This relates to the great fighter Nai Khanom Dhom who having been captured by the Burmese regained his freedom by defeating twelve of Burma's best fighters. The Burmese King of that time, Mangra, was so impressed by Nai Khanom Dhoms' technique that he was given the choice between jewels, wives or his freedom. He chose his freedom and went on to become a great hero of the Thai people. His feat was so important that the event was honoured and to this day stadiums around Thailand still honour their hero by dedicating one fight night a year to him (17 March).

The oldest confirmed record of the first true Muay Thai bouts comes from the time of King Naresuen (1590–1605) when Muay Thai became part of the military training regime. It was practised from a manual known as the *Chupasart*. This dealt with the use of weaponry as well as the empty hands and it is likely that the modern practice of Muay Thai developed from the very same book. King Naresuen practised these arts personally and actually fought in several contests. In 1577 he was declared a national hero.

During the reign of King Suriyentharathibodi (1703–09) or Pra Chao Sua (The Tiger King) as he was commonly called, Thailand was at peace, and the army, having very little to do practised Muay Thai or Dee Muay. It then worked its way into the national educational curriculum and became a national pastime, a little like football in this country only more widely practised! Every village in Thailand had its fighters and would stage prizefights regularly. Heavy gambling often led to all-or-nothing fights with serious injury and even death as a consequence! Pra Chao Sua himself was said to have taken part in these bouts defeating many local champions. He would disguise himself as a commoner and records exist that claim he visited the district of Tambol Taladguad with four of his royal guards to take part in three fights against local champions Nai Klan Madtai (Killing Fist), Nai Yai Madlek (Iron Fist) and Nai Lek Madnak (Hard Fists). The King won all three fights.

Phraya Pichai Dab Hak (also known as Nai Thongdee Fan Kao) was another legendary fighter from Uttaradit (formerly Hanka, Thongyung Province). The story starts when Phraya Pichai was a young boy and was so in love with boxing he would run away from home in order to practise. One day the famous guerrilla leader Phraya Tak held a Thai contest in the town of Tak. Nai Thongdee asked the ringmaster to find him a match and having never seen this young boxer before decided to match him against someone with little experience so that the fight would be fair and exciting. Nai Thongdee was against this idea and chose to fight the most experienced boxer in the town. It was then decided that Archarn Nai Hao, whom nobody had dared challenge, would take the fight. Archarn thought that he would make an example of this young unknown upstart. Unfortunately for Hao the tables would be turned with Thongdee soundly thrashing the great Hao in superb Muay Thai style. Having been witness to this tremendous fight, Phraya Taksin immediately asked Thongdee to serve in his guerrilla army to fight against the Burmese. As the years passed by, Thongdee proved himself again and again in the ring and eventually Phraya Taksin adopted him as his personal bodyguard. Phraya Taksin was later to become King Taksin, eventually unifying Thailand against the Burmese with the help of Thongdee. The two fought in many great battles together and it is to one particular battle that we should now turn our attention. In 1767 the capital Ayuddhaya was destroyed and with it most of the history of Thailand. The city was virtually wiped off the map of Siam and during the ferocious battle to save it Phraya Taksin managed to escape to Rayong as the city fell. Here, with the help of Thongdee, Taksin would piece together an army that would eventually put an end to Burmese aggression and therefore secure the future for Siam and the freedom of its peoples.

Thongdee, under the guidance of Phraya Taksin, won back many small towns and villages and it was during one of these battles that Thongdee was to earn the name he is now known by today. In 1773, an army under the celebrated Burmese General Bo Supla was sent to capture the city of Pichai. However, the Siamese army met them head on and in a tremendous battle led by Thongdee, the General was pushed back, his army defeated and humiliated. In the heat of the battle, at Wat Aka with Phraya Sura Sri by his side, Thongdee held aloft two swords (Sorng Maa Daab), fell from his horse, and, in order to control his fall used one of the swords to steady himself. It is said that the sword broke. However, this did not stop Thongdee who carried on regardless soundly defeating the Burmese. To honour this great victory Thongdee was given the name Phraya Pichai Dab Hak, 'Phraya Pichai of the Broken Sword'. Eventually, after 15 years of war, the Siamese under King Taksin regained their territories and Phraya Pichai stayed on as his personal bodyguard until the death of King Taksin in 1782. With the succession to the throne of Rama 1 of the Chao Phraya Chakri

Fig. 2   Statue and shrine of Phraya Pichai Daab Hak in Uttaradit.

Dynasty (the present-day dynasty of Thailand), it was decided that Phraya Pichai be rewarded for his contribution and loyalty to his King and country and continue his good work as the new King's bodyguard. The tradition at that time was that when a King died then his servants and bodyguards would die with him but King Rama made an exception in this case. Phraya Pichai was so saddened by King Taksin's death, however, that he requested to be executed. He asked King Rama to take care of his son so that he in turn would become bodyguard to the new King.

Phraya Pichai Daab Hak was executed on his own orders at the age of 41. A monument was built in his memory in 1969. This beautiful bronze statue stands proudly in front of the parliament buildings in Uttaradit and serves to remind

Fig. 3 Master Lee offers good luck before a makeshift shrine at the Phraya Pichai HQ in Birmingham.

each new generation of this amazing man's courage and loyalty. His epitaph reads: 'In memory and loving honour for the pride of our Nation'.

Modern day Thai fights are no longer as brutal as these prize fights. Gloves are worn, gumshields, protective boxes and strict rules prevent deaths in the ring. In the age of Pra Chao Sua, and not uncommonly up to 1920, it is said that boxers would bind their hands in hemp, often applying a sticky resin on which they would stick ground glass. They wore crude groin guards of tree bark or shell and there was no such thing as weight divisions or timed rounds. They would simply fight till one man collapsed!

Muay Thai was being taught in schools up till 1921 when it became prohibited due to the extent of the injuries being inflicted. The use of hemp rope continued into the 1930s when radical changes were made to the sport. The rules of international boxing were adapted and adopted, weight divisions were introduced and timed bouts became the norm and Modern Muay Thai as we know it today was born.

Elements of the traditional system can still be seen in Thailand particularly in the practice of Krabi Krabong, a weapons system from which Muay Thai eventually developed, and in the Sila and Chai ya fighting systems of which very little is known. In fact Chai ya is only practised in its original form by a very small group of individuals in Bangkok and was being taught by Acharn (Master) Thonglaw Yarlair until his recent death. Acharn Thonglaw was quite clear that the practice of Chai ya was not for sport, but is a serious and dangerous self-defence system, so does not attract the numbers of students that Muay Thai does. The practitioners still practise with hands wrapped in bandages each being over 15 metres long. Traditionally these bandages were made from the winding sheets of the dead (to scare the opponent) but the custom has been abandoned. Training the mind plays as important a role in the Chai ya fighter's routine as does the physical where the adage 'use 4 ounces to move 4 thousand pounds' is put into practice with the emphasis being on using an opponent's strength and aggression against them rather than your own brute force. With only a handful of students left it looks as if this very important part of Thailand's martial arts may die out altogether and be relegated to the history books or transform itself into a ritual dance akin to Sila, a fighting system indigenous to Thailand that is more often than not practised as a dance. It bears remarkable similarities to Silat, as practised in neighbouring Indonesia and Malaysia, and is technically just as destructive. All of these arts have one thing in common in that they are not so much defensive systems as offensive

systems. Once attacked the practitioner will immediately go on the offensive, destroying the attacker mentally and then physically with an onslaught of blows. Ask anyone who has fought a Thai Boxer. You need more than Chi or some mysterious power to damage a Muay Thai fighter.

Rituals

Ritual plays a significant part in the daily life of every Thai. From the everyday rituals of honouring the house spirits to the more elaborate public displays expressed in the Water festival, ritual is woven into the very fabric of Thai society. Without going into too much detail (and it would take a book rather than a chapter to do this), I shall attempt to explain the significance of ritual and the part it plays in the practice of Muay Thai.

Thailand, being a predominantly Buddhist country, follows traditional Buddhist practices mixed with the animistic religions of former times. Long before Buddhism arrived, the people believed in the cult of the spirits and that everything in

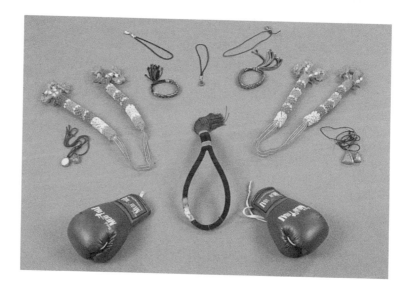

Fig. 4   A variety of amulets worn by the boxer. The Mongkon can be seen centre.

existence was home to a spirit. The people believe that every home has its own spirit guardian and hence each house has an altar that will be decked in garlands and incense, with bowls of food and other offerings placed there for the spirit. Festivals take place throughout the year where ritual has great significance, being very much part of the daily routine of life in the villages and towns. In many of these one can see old men selling amulets and charms to protect the wearer against malevolent spirits.

Indeed the boxer will wear the Praciet on the bicep as a good luck talisman. A fighter would never wear the Praciet for dress purposes; it is an object of spiritual importance and is blessed by the monks of the local 'Wat' or temple. Amulets and incantations have always played an important part in the practice of Muay Thai and some boxers fervently believe in the power attributed to these spells and charms.

The types of charms used specifically in Muay Thai are as follows:

Kongkrapan or the spell of invulnerability. This is often put in a cloth that was also placed around the neck. It could also be fashioned into a waistcoat (*Suea-yan*) and would be heavily inscribed with the spells.

Takrut is a thin sheet of metal made from either gold, silver or copper and rolled into the Praciet.

Pitsamorn is a rectangular sheet (metal or palm leaf) and put into rolled cloth. It is never folded.

Mongkon is the inscribed cloth rolled and fashioned into a headband with a tail hanging to the rear. Because it is placed on the head it is considered to be very significant in Muay Thai.

Praciet is a band of cloth traditionally red and white and is worn around the bicep during the contest. Charms are often placed within its structure.

Pirod is an amulet made from paper and is usually worn on the wrist or the finger.

Waan is a type of herb that, when used with spells, is believed to give the fighter virility, and immunity from even the hardest of strikes. It is worn in either the Mongkon or the Praciet. Some fighters would also chew this herb before the fight

Pra Krueng is a small Buddha image hidden in the Mongkon or the Praciet.

Fig. 5 The Boxer prepares himself for the Khuen Kru.

Collectively these items are classified as **Kruang Ruang** and are usually called that by most foreigners.

If a young man wishes to fight in the ring he must undergo a ritual of acceptance by a camp and a teacher. One does not simply join a boxing camp. Once a potential boxer has the verbal acceptance of a teacher he must take part in the ritual of *Khuen Kru*, which is held in front of a Buddhist shrine flanked on both sides by Thai Boxing equipment. Here he performs his vow of loyalty. The student will make the usual Buddhist offerings of flowers, incense, a strip of white cloth, candles, money and offerings of food. He will then recite the pledge of loyalty:

I come here today to pay respect to the teacher and solemnly promise to be truthful in all endeavours. I will treasure all traditions, rules, rituals and techniques that I will learn. I will never harm the reputation of the teacher or bring his teachings into disrepute. Earth, heaven and the four directions bear witness to this pledge. I ask you to help me succeed and ask for your blessing forever.

This invocation is followed by a period of meditation and *Puja* (Buddhist chants). The student is now accepted and is ready to be given his ring name. The teacher names the student according to his physical aptitude and characteristics. If for some reason the fighter loses many fights his name is regarded as inauspicious and with the help of an astrologer it will be changed.

Before a fight a boxer will always be physically prepared, but the ritual about to take place prepares him spiritually. Before entering the ring the teacher will place the Mongkon on the fighter's head. Usually made of hemp, the Mongkon is elaborately decorated and extends over the head and down the back between the shoulder blades, ending in a tassel of silk. Again, this sacred object has been blessed by the monks and each camp has its own Mongkon, some of which are very old and are therefore believed to be imbued with the power of the old fighters. The Mongkon is placed on the fighter's head by his teacher and a short prayer is said over the student. This serves as a reminder to the student that he represents not just his teacher and the camp but also the aspirations of his family and his Buddhist beliefs.

Once the fighter has entered the ring he may bow three times or touch his cornerpost three times to signify his respect for the Buddha, the Dharma (Buddhist teachings) and the Sangha (the community of monks). The number three plays a significant part in many religious rituals not just in Thailand but in many other countries around the world. For instance the Father, Son and Holy Ghost from the Christian tradition, and there are many more to be found in other religions. The fighter then moves to each cornerpost walking in an anti-clockwise direction until he has sealed the ring. Sealing the ring in such a way keeps evil spirits out and helps the fighter to seal out external distractions. From the western viewpoint it is a way to concentrate the fighter's mind. Anyone who has ever fought in the ring will attest to pre-fight nerves, and this preliminary ritual, if practised correctly, helps to contain any anxiety and tension. I use it in conjunction with a series of psychological techniques that include visualization of yourself as a Champion fighter. That is, positive internal representations of you winning the fight, experiencing all of the feelings and sounds you would associate with that event.

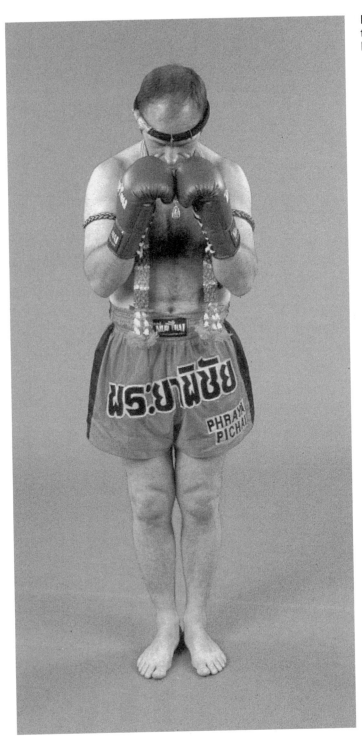

Fig. 6 Bowing three times, the Boxer shows his respect (Wai).

Fig. 7   A kneeling bow is performed.
Again this is performed three times.

Fig. 8   The Boxer now kneels in
the Khune Prone position.

Fig. 9 ... and performs sweeping movements of the arms.

Fig. 10 Having repeated this to the four directions he stands and performs similar movements ...

Fig. 11 … in a standing position, balanced on one leg.

Fig. 12 Here we see the Boxer ritually slaying the opponent.

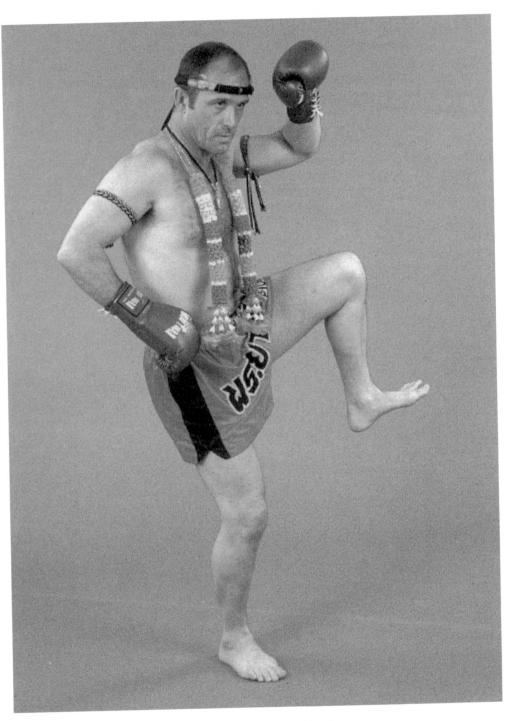

Fig. 13   Finally, leaving as the victor from the field of battle.

This ritual complete, the fighter then moves to the centre of the ring and performs the Wai Kru, or obeisance to the teacher. Here the fighter pays homage to his parents, his teacher and his training camp. The gloves are brought together at face height and the boxer bows three times usually from a squatting position.

At this stage the fighter should be in a heightened state of concentration in preparation for the Ram Muay (lit. Boxer's Dance). If done well the Ram Muay can be very beautiful to watch, sweeping movements of both the arms and legs move the body to the four directions. The number four is also quite significant to a Buddhist. The central teaching of the Buddha teaches that the road to spiritual enlightenment is through the Four noble truths: *Dukkha* (suffering), *Dukkha-samudaya* (arising of suffering), *Dukkha-niroda* (cessation of suffering) and *Dukkha-niroda-gamini-patipada* (the path leading to cessation of suffering). Again, it would take a book to explain not just these concepts, but also the many other incidences of the number four in the practice of ritual.

The Ram Muay differs from camp to camp, with each being identified by its dance. Originally this was done to prevent fighters from the same teacher fighting each other. Ardent fight fans will recognize a fighter's Ram Muay and the fighter is often applauded if the Ram Muay is performed well. Even though the dances are different one thing does remain central to each Ram Muay and that is the ancient *Khune Prone* or Brahma dance of Krabbi Krabong. Krabbi Krabong is a martial art that predates Muay Thai and it is believed that many of the traditional techniques of Muay Thai owe their existence to the Krabbi Krabong system. The Khune Prone places an emphasis on particular movements and remains unchanged in all Ram Muay. Embodying the virtues of compassion, temperance, prudence and justice it provides a balance with the hard form of the fight that is about to take place.

Whilst performing the dance the fighter is not only showing off his physical skills to the other fighter and the crowd, but is centring himself physically and, through visualization, preparing himself psychologically for the fight to come. Some of the Ram Muay are so physical they also serve as superb pre-fight warm-ups.

The boxer is under no pressure whatsoever to hurry through the ritual and has as long as it takes to complete it. Throughout the Wai Kru and the Ram Muay, music is played by a four-piece band Wong Muay, consisting of a flute (Pi'chawa), two drums of different pitches (Glong Kaek) and a pair of brass cymbals (Ching). The music serves to enhance the ritual. One has to hear it to appreciate its sound!

The band are well versed in Muay Thai and, as well as accompanying the Ram Muay, will also play during the fight, often increasing the pace of the match by speeding up the tempo!

The ritual completed, the fighter returns to his corner whereupon the teacher blows over the head of the fighter (this has ritual significance in itself), muttering a mantra (sacred words) and removing the Mongkon. The fight is about to begin!

2 Fundamental Training Principles and Techniques

Yaang Saam Khum 'Building a Firm Foundation'

If you go to any martial arts school of a high standard the first thing you will be taught are the principles of stance and footwork. Footwork is central to any martial art and, if taught correctly, will prepare the way for the development of the different techniques that are used within that system of combat. In Muay Thai this is no different. However, rather than working with a plethora of stances and postures, Muay Thai concerns itself with one stance and the appreciation of angular movement and relaxation. We do not stand for hours in a particular stance to try to develop strength or stability in that stance. By its very nature the Muay Thai stance is solid yet flexible, strong yet relaxed and prepares the body with a firm enough foundation to launch seriously powerful techniques that are proved every time a fighter enters the ring.

It is therefore important to be aware of the training drills that the Thai Boxer will use during his training regime. The most important of these is a technique known as *Yaang Saam Khum* or three strides movement. In Thailand as one would expect, this technique like many others, has its own background history and this will be inevitably linked to the Ramakien.

The Ramakien is basically the Thai version of the Ramayana, a Hindu epic that is said to be over 2,000 years old and recounts the story of the lives and adventures of a variety of gods, demons and humans. Many of the characters have connections with the Thai martial arts such as Rama, the central character in the book. Rama is Vishnu's incarnation on Earth. The son of a king, he was cheated out of his inheritance and forced into exile. Sita his wife accompanied him into the forest but was spirited away by the demon king of Ceylon and was only rescued by Rama after many battles and struggles. Eventually Rama regained his kingdom and became a great monarch combining tenderness, virtue and piety, being considerate to the people he ruled. The Ramakien has become part of the national curriculum in schools and every child can recount their favourite story when asked to do so. Other characters include Erawan the elephant, Naga the mighty serpent king and of course Hanuman the monkey god.

The Yaang Saam Khum is taught by recounting the story of Lord Siva, who, along with his wife, held a great party for his family and friends and invited all the spirits, angels and gods to be there too. During the party Lord Siva wanted to show his appreciation to certain servants of his who had worked hard and were faithful. Siva had noticed that one of his guards was particularly loyal, a giant by the name of Tatawan, and Siva asked him if there was anything he would like as a reward. Tatawan said that he would like a piece of land, 300 square miles in area

Fig. 14 A good guard stance is characterized by a high guard.

Fig. 15   Notice the curve in the spine and the balance on the balls of the feet.

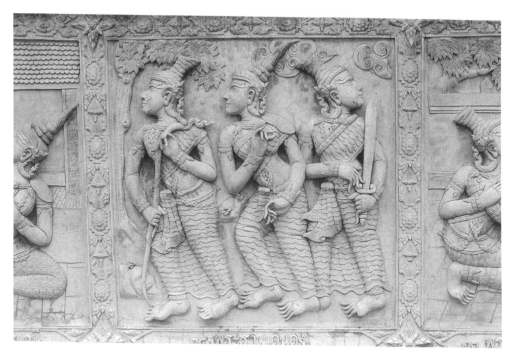

Fig. 16   A scene from the Ramakien at the ancient city of Ayuddhaya.

where he would have total control over everything that lived there. This wish was granted. However, Tatawan took advantage of this position and started to devour and destroy anything that crossed his lands. Total panic gripped the Earth and it was apparent to all that Tatawan had become a dangerous tyrant and was upsetting the natural order of things. Many of the gods begged Siva to do something to stop him and Siva heeding the complaints summoned Lord Rama from the bottom of the ocean to rid the Earth of this demon. It was usual that when Rama was summoned the result would mean death for the opponent. However, Rama was a great tactician and disguised himself as a Brahman and entered the Lands of Tatawan. As expected, Tatawan approached the Brahman threatening him with death and Rama, pretending to quake with fear,

asked that he be allowed (as a good Brahman) to perform certain rites before he died and that all he needed was a piece of land of just three strides. Tatawan was unaware of the real identity of the Brahman and allowed him the land. The Brahman then asked Tatawan if he was giving him the land so that he would later take it back? Tatawan said that it was his to give and the Brahman had his word that he could keep it.

Once the vow had been made, Rama assumed his normal identity and the earth shook as Lord Rama took three huge strides covering the whole area of Tatawan's territory. This movement is known as *Yaang Saam Khum Daern Lak* – taking back the Land.

Tatawan tried to run but was slain by Rama. There was no escape! The belief is that once a boxer has mastered the Yaang

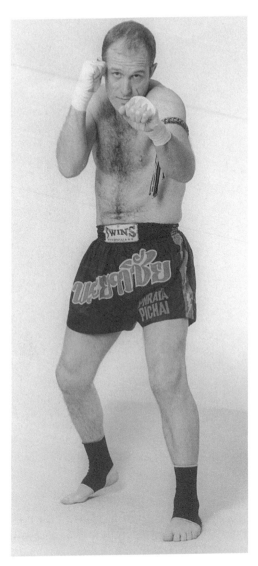

First of all we have to adopt a stance that allows for space between the legs and of course a good guard. The photographs give you a good idea of how that should be.

Standing slightly wider than a conventional western boxer the Muay Thai man can make better use of his legs and knee attacks. He keeps light on the balls of the feet, sometimes rocking from one to the other, constantly displacing his weight first on the front foot and then the rear but nearly always in motion. The Thai boxer does not bounce around in the style of a

Fig. 17 A good guard stance can vary from fighter to fighter. Here we see the lead hand slightly lower.

Saam Khum his opponent has no means of escape and will be beaten.

So this might work for a god but what about us?

Just how does the Yaang Saam Khum work?

Fig. 18 The stance is balanced and the fighter starts to move forward ...

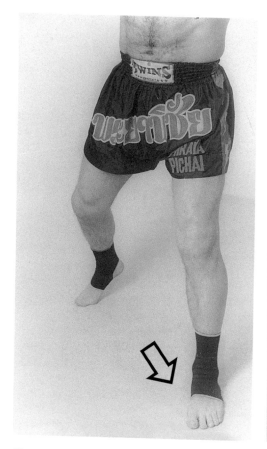

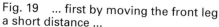

Fig. 19   ... first by moving the front leg a short distance ...

Fig. 20   ... and then bringing the rear leg into position.

traditional western boxer. He wishes to conserve his energy and not dissipate it needlessly! Any forward motion with the lead leg is recovered by the back leg so at no point must he leave the rear leg stretched out. If this is done there will be a dramatic decrease in the amount of power he may generate. By adopting this natural stance he may make full use of the hips allowing them to turn through 180 degrees in some cases – which brings me to my next point. Power comes from the correct use of the hips. It does not come from the arms or the legs exclusively. Without a

relaxed and comfortable stance the hips cannot be rotated freely, thus depriving the boxer of power.

Moving up the body we see the boxer has his torso square onto the attacker, keeping his hips in a chambered position and his front knee pointing forward. This keeps the front leg strong in case it is attacked by low kicks from the opponent. The spine is curved and the body takes on a slightly arched appearance. The lead hand (in this case the left) is placed away from the face serving as both a rangefinder and a weapon. The elbow is hanging

Fig. 21 Some Boxers favour a 'Southpaw' stance.

loosely down to protect the vulnerable rib area. The right hand is placed by the right side of the face protecting the eyebrow, jaw-line, cheekbone and the vulnerable neck area. Again the elbow can be seen to be protecting the ribs. Finally the head is dropped loosely forward with the boxer gazing through the eyebrows presenting less of the 'soft parts' of the face to the attacker and the spine is therefore curved, pulling the abdomen in, thereby protecting the ribs. This then is the basic stance from which the fighter may launch his attacks or defend himself against attacks. There will always be slight variations on this but that is to be expected. We are not all the same body type. Some may have longer legs, some of you may be left-handed and favour what is known as the 'southpaw' stance. This is simply a reverse of the instructions above and is considered awkward to fight against. Of course, that all depends on your training method!

These important criteria, as long as they are observed, should give you stability, and hence the ability to move in all directions smoothly and quickly.

Basic Movement

When moving, the boxer should always slide the feet either toward the target or

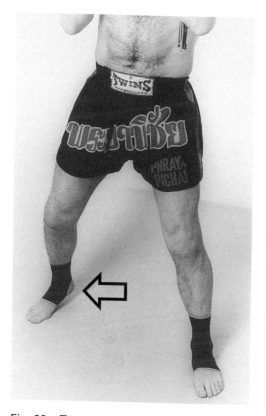

Fig. 22   To move to the right, step with the right foot first ...

Fig. 23   ... followed quickly by the left foot.

29

Fig. 24   Other guard positions can be adopted.

Fig. 25 Here we see a high shin guard and cross block.

observe the criteria already outlined above. It is important to maintain balance and be fluid in our movement and economical too. Move enough to avoid the attack and no more than that. If in a left stance and you intend moving to the left, step off first with the left foot with the right following swiftly after. Moving to the right means we must step off with the right foot, followed then by the left. Always ensure that your front, or lead, leg keeps lifting to prepare for movement, kicking or

Fig. 26 The same guard from the front.

away from the target. The movement should be fluid and the hips should follow the same line. When moving forwards the front leg moves first with the rear leg following quickly behind. Moving backwards means sliding the back leg away first and following with the front leg. Always maintain space between the legs ensuring that the stance is not too long or narrow. Always keep light on the balls of the feet, keeping the rear heel raised at all times. This allows for explosive push-off in the direction of the target. Bodyweight is therefore placed forward and onto the toes as you move.

The boxer can also move from side to side to avoid a blow. Again we must blocking. It also means that your opponent will be less likely to come steaming in on the attack. What could be simpler!

Angular Movement

Understand this section on footwork and you will have learned the most valuable technique in any martial art. It will prepare you for any eventuality and is the concept underlying what I understand and teach in martial arts. At first it may seem difficult to apply but, through a little practice, you should be doing it without thinking – which is the general idea anyway! When you are attacked from the front you have a couple of choices. You either back off (in self-protection this puts you back in the same situation as when it started) or you confront, hold your ground and attack. The best method, and it's the one I advocate both in the ring and in the street, is to move forward and attack. Psychologically it is the most difficult choice to make and not the one most of us are conditioned to do. Physically it can be damaging if you are not sure about what to do on the 'way in'. A well-trained fighter can simply wade in, crashing through the attacker's defences, surprising him and therefore taking advantage of the situation. That's one way in. The other, is to move in but at 45 degrees to the intended target. This keeps us at close range allowing us to use some of the most devastating techniques we have but avoiding excessive physical contact with the attacker. Psychologically, it is a little easier to gain confidence in moving forward when attacked because it is unlikely that we will be hit. Constant practice will develop a habit of moving in when confronted rather than flinching backward. For a boxer this is very important. There are three distinct phases to bear in mind when using angular footwork:

1. Evade the attack moving forward and to the left or right
2. Control and neutralize the attacker's limb/limbs
3. Damage or strike attacker's vulnerable areas

This is Yaang Saam Khum or three strides movement in greater detail. This drill will prepare you for tactical footwork as used in the ring. This gives you the ability to control the movement of your opponent in and around the ring forcing them into a corner or against the ropes where they literally run out of space and, like Tatawan, are devoured.

It is possible to practise footwork drills in isolation but it is always better to practise in conjunction with actual techniques (punches, kicks and so on). Training in Thailand means that you practise footwork and little else for your first three days! It is also best to train with a partner, preferably one that will not be afraid of trying to hit you (keeping a certain amount of control). If you are to develop effective footwork, realism must be the name of the game. Remember also, that reading about it is one thing and doing it another. Find a Muay Thai teacher who understands the Yaang Saam Khum and learn from them. You will be surprised at how many teachers will not have even heard about this technique. However, if they are reputable they will know it. It is the basis of Muay Thai.

Figs 24–27 on pages 30–33 show the variety of basic guard positions that a fighter might adopt.

Now that we have a better understanding of footwork we will take a look at the equipment and techniques of Muay Thai. These are the basic techniques upon which you will, with the help of this book, and with the help of a qualified

Fig. 27 The Wedge Block and Salute Position is used when moving into close range.

Fig. 28   Consider checking your fighting distance by the prudent use of the Front Kick.

instructor, discover more about the art of Muay Thai. Amongst these fundamentals the most important one of all is the understanding of Range Finding. Movement without an understanding of distance is pointless. Range Finding allows you to maintain:

Balance
Stability
Power
Speed
Control
Technique

In order to make the best use of the hands, elbows, knees, shins and feet, we need to move to a position where they will operate at their most effective. It is no good, for example, reaching for the opponent or trying to punch the opponent when he is out of reach. It would be better to use a kick. Our main concern is to conserve energy, and be economical in our movements. In the ring you must pace yourself, and this requires economy of motion. In the street it could mean the difference between life and death so we must learn to use the correct tool for the job. To get the job done efficiently we use our footwork. This allows us to operate at any one or all of the following three ranges.

Long Range
Medium Range
Short Range

Fig. 29   Both fighters stand at their optimum distance ...

Cross. Other techniques such as Uppercuts, Hooks, Backfists, Palm Heel Strikes, Ridge Hand Strikes and combinations can be used at this range. However, the important thing to remember is that all of these techniques allow you to get into a position where you can move in to the most effective range of all, both in terms of self-protection or sport.

Short Range: This is where Muay Thai comes into its own. At this range you have the opportunity of using the most powerful weapons in the body. The Elbows and the Knees. Used in a variety of ways, and in conjunction with the hands, the fighter can dominate the opposition. Used in conjunction with Clinch Work, the head and shoulders can also be used. This is the range all fighters should be capable of working. To gain control requires knowledge of close-range fighting.

Long Range: Here we are at kicking distance, and can employ a variety of kicks. To the Thai boxer this means Front Kicks and Roundhouse Kicks. Both types of kick can be delivered high, medium or low and make maximum use of the hip to generate power. Aimed at the head, body or legs these can cause considerable damage; using the ball of the foot or the toes for the front kick and the shin in the case of the roundhouse kick. This is your optimum distance. A Thai boxer usually trains to stay at this range early on in their training.

Medium Range: This is the area in which the hands come into their own, although to a limited extent the Thai-style Long Knee technique may also be used very effectively. The lead hand is suitably positioned for a jab (a short stabbing movement), and the right hand for a right

Fig. 30   ... which is easily checked by using a jab.

Fig. 31 You know you are at close range when it is possible to hold the opponent and knee them.

As we progress through this chapter we will learn how to use all of the above techniques and the 'tricks' associated with them. That's the easy part! I call them tricks because it doesn't take long to actually learn them. Anyone can pick them up in a very short space of time. The most difficult thing however is learning how to make them work effectively and this requires good footwork.

Before we take a look at the striking techniques themselves we need to know where it is we should strike to create the effect we desire. These areas are known as *Jot Aun* or Vital Points.

Vital Points (*Jot Aun*)

Generally speaking, if the human body is hit hard enough, then an opponent will be injured. However, it is important to note that certain areas of the body are subject to damage more easily than others. Outlined below are the traditionally attacked areas of the body as taught in Thailand.

Crown of the head. This is often struck using an elbow strike and is considered extremely dangerous.

Temple. In Thai it is known as *Tat Daok Mai* and again the elbow is the best weapon with which to attack this very sensitive area.

Eyebrow. Using the elbow to this area means a serious cut can occur and therefore impair the vision of the boxer. The fighter may also continually rub this area with the glove to keep the cut open once it is affected.

Eye. This target is usually attacked with the elbow being used in a downward fashion aimed at the eyebrow. In self-protection the eye can be attacked with the thumb or fingers.

Nose. Any type of punch or elbow strike results in pain and bleeding and in severe cases the nose may be broken. This will not usually stop the fight but causes swelling and closing of the eyes.

Jaw. The elbow or punches aimed at the jaw when on target will usually result in a KO. It is also possible to break the jaw in extreme cases.

Chin. A straight punch or an uppercut punch/elbow to the chin usually results in a KO.

Adam's apple. A seriously dangerous area to attack with any weapon. Can cause death. To attack this area in competition is considered a foul.

Nape of the neck. A kick to this area will cause a KO. Elbows too have been known to be used against this area.

Collar Bone. The elbow dropped down onto the collarbone can break it and cause an internal injury to the lung.

Heart. An elbow, short punch or knee one inch below the nipple is very painful and in ancient times it was not unheard of for a fighter to be killed striking this area. However, the wearing of gloves prevents this ever happening now.

Solar plexus. Punches, elbows and knees are very effective used here and usually end with a KO.

Bladder. A well placed front kick or knee to this area can be serious. Usually a KO or pain is encountered when striking this area. This is one of the main targets of Muay Thai.

Ribs. If the floating ribs are attacked they can be broken and cause a great deal of pain. A roundhouse kick, knee or uppercut elbow or punch are the most commonly used types of attack to this area.

Groin. Although not widely known, this area is a legal target in Muay Thai com-

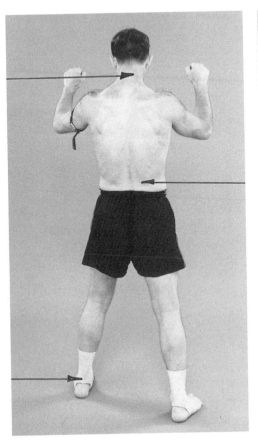

Fig. 32   Vital points rear view.

Fig. 33   Vital points front view.

petition and can obviously cause a great deal of pain.

Thigh. Weakened by low kicks the boxer may suffer muscle cramps and stiffening of the leg.

Knee. Easily damaged and weakened by kicking or blocking.

Kidney. A well-aimed knee, round-house kick or elbow can cause a KO in extreme cases, pain in others.

Achilles tendon. A strike with a low kick (used in a sweeping motion) can cause great pain and in extreme cases prevent the boxer from remaining on his feet.

Instep. The top of the foot is a particularly sensitive area especially when struck with the elbow or shin. This is done when blocking a mid/low-level roundhouse kick.

Natural Weapons of Muay Thai

This section will cover all of the basic techniques of Muay Thai and will give suggested combinations for you to practise.

However, it is important to be familiar with the variety of weapons used in Muay Thai. These are as follows:

1. Fists
2. Elbows
3. Knees
4. Legs
5. Grappling

When punching, kicking and striking with any of these weapons, coordinate your breathing with the technique. As a general rule breathe out on exertion, in other words, as you extend the technique. The Thai have their own style when doing this and the strange sounds of 'eeesh', 'oiyee' and 'ooos' are heard during a training session. Before discussing the attacking techniques of Muay Thai it is important to take into account the types of defence employed by the boxer.

Defensive Methods of Muay Thai

The Thai boxer employs four types of defence. Each of the following are in descending order of importance and are judged as such in a fight.

1. Evasion
This is a priority for the boxer and can be practised in a variety of ways, but however it is done, it is performed in such a way as to keep you close to the opponent without compromising yourself. Backward steps, evasion to the side and even tucking the body are various types of evasion.

2. Blocking
An attack can be blocked with the edge of

Fig. 34 Evade the kick by stepping back or tucking the body.

39

Fig. 35   Lift the lead leg straight up to block an approaching low kick.

the forearm or the shin. A kick may also be jammed by stamping against the incoming thigh, knee or hip. When blocking with the arm it is important to ensure that not only the arm is used but the elbow should also be brought to bear onto the opponent's instep. This creates damage and prevents further use of this leg in kicking. The shin block is traditionally used in Muay Thai and, rather than strike the opponent's

Fig. 36 Catching the front kick and then lifting it will pull the opponent off balance.

shin, it is better to try and strike the opponent's instep. Again this prevents further attacks done with this leg.

3. Grabbing

When attacked with a roundhouse kick it is often possible to absorb the blow and, catching hold of it, pull the attacker off balance and counter-attack with a kick or technique of your own. Sometimes it may be possible to lift the leg and throw the opponent onto the canvas. This also works especially well against the *teep* or front kick.

4. Absorbing

The last possible means of defence must of course be absorption of the attack (*see* Fig. 37). This is dangerous and can often lose a fighter the match, because of injury or KO. It is used as a tactic but obviously puts you at higher risk and is therefore judged as such.

It is now time to look at the striking techniques that make Muay Thai the distinctive art it is today. The techniques explained and demonstrated can be done alone, with a partner, on the pads or the heavy bags. All are tried and tested and there are no extraneous techniques. In this publication we have steered clear of many of the 'spectacular' techniques of the art and have concentrated on the 'basics'.

Kicking

It is kicking that distinguishes Muay Thai from traditional boxing and the Thai uses his kicks in a very different way from his other martial arts counterparts.

For a kick to be effective it must be balanced and it must travel through the target. To maintain equilibrium the supporting leg must be in a controlled state. When kicking, keep the supporting leg slightly bent and relaxed, allowing the foot to turn freely on the ball. Before a kick always chamber the leg to the correct position. There are a number of kicks used in Muay Thai. We intend looking at only the most basic.

Fig. 37   As a last resort a fighter may absorb the attack!

Front Kick (*Teep Drong*)

Lift the lead leg to the chamber position and then deliver the kick in one of two ways:

a. With full hip flexion
b. With a snapping movement.

The ball of the foot is normally used but can be more damaging if the toes of the foot are jabbed in to the target (*Teep Dueh Son*). Preferred targets include the thigh, pelvis, bladder and chin.

Standing in a left lead leg stance, lift the knee of the right leg to a chamber position directly in front of the body. With a light hopping motion forward drive the hips and the leg forward in a straight line. If you wish to use full hip flexion, angle the foot slightly with the toes pointing at 45 degrees inward pushing the right hip into the technique. For some people this can be a more powerful way to kick. The Teep can be done with the right leg as well as the left and the lead leg is often used like that of a boxer's jab (snapped into the target), keeping the opponent at a distance and setting him up for a further attack.

This technique can be practised with a partner with or without pads and also practised on the heavy bags.

Defence against Front Kicks

The obvious defence against this type of kick is to move out of its path. But rather than retreat from the kick it is better to catch the kick as shown on page 41. An alternate type of grab is shown on page 45. Once you have done this you are now in a position to counter-attack with a number of combinations.

A skilled fighter could also slip just inside the kick (this takes practice!) grabbing the leg with your left arm and pushing the opponent off balance with the right hand.

The best defence against a push kick is to be aware that it is about to be launched and step in, pre-empting the technique with a counter of your own.

Front kicks may be caught with either the left or right hand and then lifting the kick slightly pulls the opponent off balance allowing you to move in with a counter-attack.

Finally, and only if your judgment of distance is accurate, you may take the kick whilst slightly retreating, thereby diminishing the power of the kick, and then countering. Remember, a well-aimed Teep to the bladder can sometimes end in a KO.

Another type of front kick is the peck kick or *Neb*. This is a short stabbing type of kick aimed at various parts of the anatomy, mainly the legs, bladder or chin.

Roundhouse Kick (*Dtae Wiang*)

Not to be confused with the roundhouse-kick of Karate or Kung fu. This is considered to be *the* kick of Muay Thai. Targets include the head, neck, arms, ribs, kidneys, thighs, knees, ankles and calves. When thrown correctly and targeted at the thighs it can be devastating. The power is generated by lifting the leg to the chamber position, and by using a step across the front of the opponent, the leg is released and the supporting leg is allowed to spin on the ball of the foot. You must release the hips and let it go. Because of the destructive capabilities of this kick it is not possible to strike with the foot and hence the boxer must use his shin as the weapon. This is generally conditioned by long hours spent kicking the heavy bag and the Thai long mitts. In Thailand, kicking banana trees can achieve the same effect! (If you can find one, that is!)

Fig. 38   Starting from a good guard position ...

Fig. 39   ... Steve lifts his lead leg to the 'chamber' position.

Fig. 40   Snapping the front kick into the opponents bladder (Teep).

Fig. 41   He then brings the leg back to the chamber position before placing it back on the ground.

Fig. 42   Here we see Jim catching the front kick with an inside grab.

The kick can either cut down into the target, cut across horizontally or cut up into the target. It should be practised each way. Be aware that when kicking below the waist, kick across, when aiming into the rib area, cut the kick up at an angle, and when kicking to the neck or head area, strike down. Note the position of the arm as shown in the photographs. This is vitally important in protecting you against counter-attacks to the jaw, and has a secondary gain for you in terms of adding more power to the kick.

Fig. 43   A well aimed Teep to the bladder can cause a KO.

Defence against the Roundhouse Kick

As a first option always evade. Step back with the lead leg and bounce back into kicking range immediately striking the opponent. If you don't have the time to try this technique, your next natural move would be a block.

The practice of using the shin as a blocking implement cannot be emphasized enough. Once the shin is conditioned it is extremely effective and can be practised in

Fig. 44 The Roundhouse Kick can cut across the opponent ...

a number of ways, either with the lead leg or rear leg. It can be performed with a jump, with a skip, or from a stationary position. Never attempt to stop a full power low roundhouse using the arm. Do not drop the arm. I've seen more than one arm broken in this fashion and it also leaves the boxer's head exposed to a possible attack. To perform the block, lift the leg vertically with the toes preferably pointed up. For kicks to the head it is possible to cover the head with the upper arm and go with the kick but, again, an appreciation of timing and distance are required to pull

this off without injury. The more experienced fighters can grab the incoming leg and upset the balance of the aggressor. Apart from simply avoiding the kick one can also use a push kick to the top of the thigh or into the hip of the attacker's kicking leg. If your timing is accurate, a well-placed Teep to the mid-section of the opponent will literally stop them in their tracks. It might even knock them off balance causing them to fall. Done correctly this can disable the attacker. You are simply stopping the attack before it even gains momentum.

Fig. 45 ... or up and into the opponent. Here we see Jim defend against Bob's Jab with a Roundhouse Kick.

Fig. 46 Jim attacks Wayne's lead leg with a Low Roundhouse Kick.

Fig. 47   A shin block protects the Boxer from Low Kicks.

Fig. 48   Here Woz catches Steve's Kick and counters immediately with a Low Roundhouse Kick to Steve's knee.

Fig. 49 Catching the kick like this allows you to push the opponent off or even attack the opponent with knees as you hold them.

Fig. 50 Blocking a mid-level kick with the forearm allows you to stay in range for a powerful counter. You may also jab your elbow onto the attacker's foot.

Spinning Heel Kick (*Choraked Faad Haang*)

Literally means 'Crocodile Whips his Tail' and is usually performed only when your roundhouse kick to the head misses its target. You continue to move round using the momentum to spin your body and thence your other leg around in a spinning fashion. You therefore hit the opponent in a circular fashion striking with the heel of what was the support leg.

Rear Thrust Kick (*Teep Dan Lang*)

This is not often seen in the ring as it means turning your back on the opponent. These kicks are only done when a roundhouse kick misses its target and spins the body around. To practise this technique simply turn your back to your opponent, chamber the leg in the same way as for the front kick and thrust out to the rear with the heel.

Fig. 51 The rarely seen Rear Thrust Kick.

Defence

Simply side-stepping this kick puts the opponent at a distinct disadvantage. As this kick is easy to spot you will have more than enough time to set up a counter-attack with a low kick to the support leg or simply wait until the opponent turns and move in with any hand, elbow or knee attack.

Side Thrusting Kick

It is very rare to see this kick used in the ring but it is nevertheless practised in some camps in Thailand. When a roundhouse kick misses the target it is often dropped down onto the ground and turned into a side-kick of this sort. Pushed into the target area in much the same way as the front kick, the body is turned to the side and the leg pushed or stamped out into the target. Used mainly against the body, it is quite an easy attack to stop.

As with all kicks it is important to keep the supporting leg relaxed, thereby allowing it to travel freely through its whole range of motion.

Knee Attacks (*Kow*)

Knee attacks are one of the most powerful natural weapons we have and are used very effectively by Thai Boxers. Practised in a number of ways the knee is a long-range weapon (in the case of the Jumping Knee), a medium-range weapon (in the case of the Long Knee) and a short-range weapon (when used in the clinch). It is either thrust into the target or snapped onto the target utilizing the front or top of the knee as its striking area. Again, full use of the hips is required to make this an effective weapon. The knees are usually used in conjunction with clinchwork, when the opponent is held and drawn onto the oncoming knee. Target areas include the

Fig. 52 Knee attacks are one of the most powerful ways a Thai Boxer can win his fights.

thighs, ribs, bladder, head and face. From the point of view of self-defence the groin makes an easy target although attacks to this area are illegal in competition.

Front Knee (*Kao Drong*)

Again working from the left lead leg stance, preferably in the clinch, simply lift the right knee up and into the target with a stepping motion forwards. The hands are placed in front of the upper body, providing adequate defence against any counter-attacks and the boxer should come up onto the toes of the supporting leg. Body position can vary from a forward leaning to a leaning back position. These are both favoured methods in Thailand and the photographs show the possible variations.

Fig. 53 The left knee can be jabbed into the opponent as he moves forwards.

Fig. 54 Controlling the head of the opponent Clyde drives a right knee into the opponent's mid-section.

Fig. 55 The Long Knee is pushed into the opponent rather than snapped.

Long Knee (*Ng Kao*)

The Long Knee is both defence and attack in one. Attention must be paid to balance when training in this. The Long Knee is usually used to attack the solar plexus or stomach region. It can be changed from a short-range weapon into a long-range one simply by extending the leg and converting it to a Front Kick. When the Long Knee is lifted it serves as protection for the groin and body area and can be converted to a shin block easily. Many fighters will lean well back to gain maximum extension when performing this knee. However, this can be its main weakness, as balance will be easily disrupted.

Fig. 56   The Roundhouse Knee is curved around and into the opponent's floating ribs.

Fig. 57   The Curved Knee is brought into play only in the Clinch. The targets include the kidney area as well as the body and legs.

Roundhouse Style Knee (*Dtae Kao*)

The leg having been lifted to the chamber position shown, it is then pushed up into the target area with a slight hop or a step. Target areas include the ribs, bladder and thighs. When you become proficient in clinchwork it is also possible to set up your opponent for an attack to the head. To perform well, think of throwing a Roundhouse Kick but do not allow the leg to follow through. Again ensure that your guard hand is pushed forward with the attacking knee. If the attack is performed with the right then the right hand should be forward. If the left knee is used, push forward the left hand.

Curved Knee

The knee is lifted up and out away from the body and moved in and strikes the opponent's limbs, body or even the head. Sometimes performed in conjunction with a hop and hip twist, this technique is a lot more powerful than it looks. It is easily practised on a heavy bag when struck with the inside surface of the knee and is used a great deal when practising the waist clinch.

Fig. 58 Jab the Rabbit Knee into the thigh with a rapid motion.

Rabbit Knee (*Kow Kratai*)

These are short stabbing knees often performed when in the clinch. They are used to good effect against the thighs and inner knee joint area and can be very painful.

Other types of knees such as Jumping and Flying Knees are used in Muay Thai but are considered to be more advanced and are not covered in this basic manual.

Knees are best practised with a partner. Hold onto the head and neck of your partner and thrust the knee into the long mitt as shown. Your partner can set up a rhythm by moving the pad from left to right, whilst you skip or step through, jabbing knees in from left to right. This exercise, when practised correctly, is an excellent stamina exercise. Your partner can increase the pressure simply by pulling against your resistance giving it a hint of realism. It is sometimes wise to wear the belly shield along with the pads for extra protection.

Always practise the knees with care as they will very easily injure your partner if misdirected.

RIGHT: Fig. 59   The Long Pads and Belly Shield should be used to develop skill in the use of Clinchwork and Knees.

BELOW: Figs 60 & 61   The padman can be turned and pulled as alternate Knees strike the pads.

Fig. 62   From a 'Southpaw' stance we can see clearly the twisting action of the wrist as the punch approaches the opponent.

Defence against Knee Attacks

When defending against a knee attack remember the four types of defensive measures. Evade, Block, Grab but don't try to Absorb the knee. Certainly not at close range! Caution must be exercised in training as the knee is a short-range weapon and is very difficult to spot. However, the best defence against the knee in any situation is to simply pull, or push the

Fig. 63 Notice the protective shoulder position as Jim attacks with a Left Jab.

opponent off balance! The forthcoming chapter on clinchwork will give a clearer indication as to what works best at close range. Pushing your shin into the path of the knee is another method of defence.

Hands (*Dtoi*) or Basic Boxing (*Chok Lum*)

The hands act as a bridge between the kicks and the more lethal elbows and knees. It is therefore very important to use them effectively. To be effective means to have power and speed. To gain these qualities requires good technique and relaxation.

The mechanics of punching are as follows, and although they should be followed strictly I realize that we are not all capable of being textbook boxers. It is the job of a coach to make the best use of the material available and adhere to as many of these principles as possible.

The punch should always follow the feet and therefore the principles on stance and movement should be practised constantly. Power comes from the rotation of the hips; it is simply released through the fist and arm. Always twist the fist at the end of the punch, corkscrewing that little extra energy from the technique and allowing it to penetrate the target. Always retract the arm along the same path back to its guard position. Always aim through the target. When striking with the fist always hit with the first two knuckles keeping the wrist straight as shown.

Fig. 64 The boxer on the right uses a 'slip' to defend against a Jab.

Fig. 65 The boxer on the left uses a 'Layback'.

Fig. 66   It is possible to 'catch' or 'parry' the attack.

The Jab (*Yaeb*)

The Jab is a straight punch thrown off the lead hand into the opponent's head or body. Directed at the head, it can and should be used as a knockout punch. When training the Jab, go for power and speed, sometimes even flicking it out to annoy the opponent. Again, turning the hips away from the punch gives greater momentum and power. Step forward slightly with the punch, twisting the fist in, as it reaches the target. Raise the shoulder of the punching hand slightly giving cover to the jaw. The right hand should remain in its covering position close by the right side of the face.

Defence

Using angular footwork to either the right or left of the punch (slipping) gives you time to set up your counter. This could be a Roundhouse Kick, Knee Strike, Clinch or an Elbow. The boxing technique of a layback is also a useful technique but can sometimes leave you open to leg attacks.

It is also possible to parry or catch the punch as it reaches its target. Ducking can be used but bear in mind that should you duck too low you are likely to get caught out with a knee to the head!

Straight Right or Right Cross (*Dtoi Kwaa*)

Often thrown in conjunction with the left Jab, this is a very powerful technique if the principles are followed. Ensure that the punch moves in a straight line to the target letting the hips take the punch out and the rear leg (heel raised) driving the body forward into the target. Remember the sequence:

Fig. 67 When 'ducking' watch out for the opponent's knee.

Fig. 68 Note the position of the rear foot as the Right Cross is thrown towards the opponent.

Fig. 69 The boxer on the right 'slips' the punch by stepping off to the right. As he moves he could throw a Right Cross as a counter.

1. drive forward off the rear leg
2. turn the hips into the punch
3. turn the shoulders
4. extend the right arm.

When retracting the punch, come back along the same path quickly and, as you punch, ensure that the left hand is close to the left side of the face. There is often the tendency in beginners to lift the elbow of the right arm prior to the punch. When coaching, keep a close eye on this to prevent it from happening. You are telegraphing your intention to the opponent.

The Right Cross, like the Jab, can be thrown both to the head or the body and can be practised on focus pads and heavy bags.

attacking arm slipping either to the left or right leaves you in an advantageous position from which to launch a variety of counters.

Stepping Punch (*Mat Drong*)

From left stance, step through with the right leg releasing the right arm toward the target. The punch should connect as the foot touches the ground. Often used against an opponent who has been knocked or has stumbled backwards.

Defence

Sidestepping and backing off are the best methods of defence against this punch. It is easy to see it coming and therefore can be easy to avoid. Most straight punches can also be stopped by use of the Cross Block.

Uppercuts (*Mat At*)

Essentially a short-range weapon used to the jaw and body region. Here the palm of the punching hand faces the boxer and the arm travels upward being kept bent at 90 degrees. The path it follows is perpendicular and works at its best when driven into and up the centreline of the opponent. Flexibility of the hips is required for this technique to be at its most powerful and is well worth working on regularly. Best practised on the focus mitts.

The Right Uppercut should follow this sequence.

Fig. 70   The Wedge Block is a highly effective offensive as well as defensive technique.

Defence

Ducking, Slipping and the Layback technique can all be used against the Right Cross as well as the Wedge Block. The left arm moves quickly inside the attack forming a wedge and blocking with the forearm. An immediate counter with the same elbow would be a natural counter-attack here. It is also possible to step in and stop the attack by use of the Cross Block. This diverts the attack by sending it down the defending arm. Finally, rolling under the

1. Drop the right shoulder turning the hips to the left
2. Allow punch to travel up the opponent's centreline
3. Right leg drives the hips up into the target
4. Palm of the right hand should be facing in toward you
5. Keep the left hand close to the left side of the head.

Fig. 71   The Cross Block protects the fighter against most types of attack to the head.

Fig. 72   The Right Uppercut is a close-range technique. Move in close to get the best results.

The Left Uppercut is based on the same principles, but follows a steeper path. Therefore it has less leverage at your disposal to generate the power. What we do however is to compensate for this by using the explosive drive of the left hip and leg. This is often used against an opponent moving in, in an attempt to apply the clinch.

1. Drop the left shoulder pushing the hips to the right
2. Allow the punch to travel up the centre-line
3. Push up with the left leg and hip
4. Palm should face toward you at end of technique
5. Ensure right hand protects right-hand side of face.

Fig. 74   Defend the Right Uppercut to the body by use of the Wedge Block.

Fig. 73   The Left Uppercut is best used as the opponent moves in for the clinch.

Defence

Layback, Retreating and Elbow Blocks are good methods of avoiding this technique as is the Wedge Block. If a Right Uppercut is coming in, simply drop your left forearm down into the crook of the opponent's elbow keeping the forearm stiff. Right hand is now ready to counter.

Left and Right Hooks (*Kwaa Hook, Saai Hook*)

In boxing this is considered the most dangerous punch of all. Coming from outside

Fig. 75 Always try to cut down on the jaw when throwing the Right Hook.

the defender's field of view it can easily slip inside the defender's glove and catch the jaw. Fundamentally a short-range technique, it is usually neglected by the Thai boxer in favour of the elbow. But this does not mean that the Thai boxer should not practise it. Variations in the position of the striking fist are shown dependent upon the level of the Hook (to the head or the body). The sequences for the right and left are as follows:

1. Stepping into range, twist the right hip
2. Followed by the right shoulder
3. The bent right arm continues in an arc

4. Transfer body weight to left leg
5. Twisting the fist as it hits the target.

For the Left Hook, one simply reverses the points above.

Defence

Layback, Wedge Block and Retreating are the best ways to deal with this type of attack. One of the best ways of dealing with this type of attack is to use the Swan Neck Block. Move in against the opponent as they deliver the Hook, catch the arm at the bicep and tricep and either pull in to clinch or strike with the Elbow or Knee.

Elbow Techniques (*Sawk*)

A typical and popular technique of Muay Thai, the Elbow, is said to be the most powerful weapon a boxer possesses. It can be used long range with a jump but is best used at short range particularly when in the clinch or moving into the clinch. Because the Elbow causes the majority of cutting injuries in the ring, it is important to remember the position of the guard hand and, when training, practise the techniques with care. The Elbow is used in a number of ways.

Side Elbow (*Kahng Sawk*)

From the left lead leg stance the Left Elbow is directed toward the head in a short snapping movement, the hand of the attacking arm being kept open and relaxed throughout. Allow the hips to twist fully. The sequence is the same as that of the Hook. The Right Elbow is performed in much the same way as the Right Hook with the hips starting the technique and the Elbow completing it. Again the target would be the head (*see* Fig. 84) and in some cases the body. It should be practised

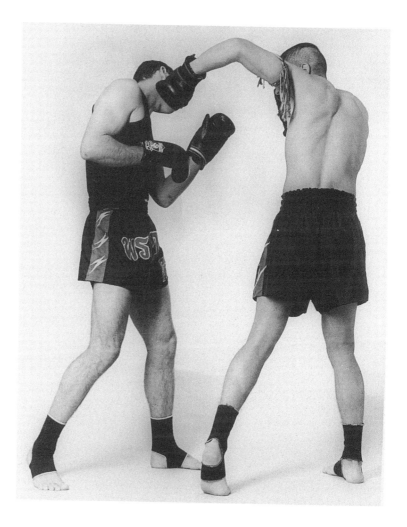

Fig. 76 The Left Hook should also strike in a downward arc.

Fig. 77   From a guard position ...

Fig. 78   ... Woz (left) steps in and catches the Right Hook with a Swan Neck Block.

Fig. 79   Reaching through with the right hand he pulls the head ...

Fig. 80   ... down and onto the knee.

Fig. 81   Jumping elbows like this
Side Elbow ...

Fig. 82   and the downward strike
are exceptionally difficult to defend
against.

Fig. 83 The open hand position is vitally important when throwing a Side Elbow. Keep it open and relaxed for best results.

either on the pads or the heavy bag. Thai teachers say that you should imagine that the Elbow is being used like a knife. In other words, short cutting-like movements.

Defence

If you can avoid the Elbow then do so! If not, your only real chance is to cover and counter simultaneously using the Wedge Block (*see* Fig. 85) or stepping inside, stop the Elbow by punching or jamming the shoulder of the attacking limb. Once blocked, most types of elbow can be countered with a grab and slip into clinch.

Uppercut Elbow (*Sawk Hud*)

Slipping inside the guard, the Right and Left Uppercut or Rising Elbow, is aimed at the chin and performed with a snapping motion upward on the centreline of the body (*see* Fig. 87). Similar to the mechanics of the Uppercut Punch, it is far more powerful. The hand of the attacking elbow should be thrown over the shoulder. It is imperative however, that the other arm is protecting the face and head against attack.

Defence

The best defence against this attack is to evade. It is impossible to block effectively or safely.

Diagonal or Cutting Elbow (*Sawk Chieng*)

A cross between the Side Elbow and the Uppercut Elbow, this is the most powerful of the static elbow techniques. The technique either cuts up at 45 degrees or down the same diagonal as shown. Used on both the left and right this is very difficult to defend against. Again, it is important to use the hips and throw the attacking hand over the opposite shoulder.

Spinning Elbow

This elbow has tremendous power when used correctly. When an opponent stumbles or is temporarily disabled by an attack, the boxer simply steps across the attack and lifting the left arm in a high arc co

Fig. 84   As the opponent clinches, strike out with a cutting action.

Fig. 86   Here we see the boxer simultaneously blocking and countering with a clinch.

Fig. 85   The Wedge Block is the best type of cover against any type of Elbow attack.

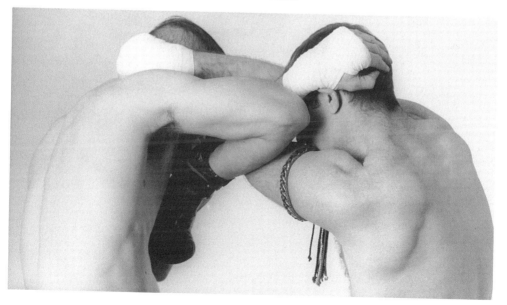

Fig. 87   A sharp twist of the hip adds even more power to your Uppercut Elbow.

TOP RIGHT: Fig. 88   Sometimes a short snapping motion will have the same effect.

RIGHT: Fig. 89   The Diagonal Elbow cuts down and into the eyebrow of the opponent.

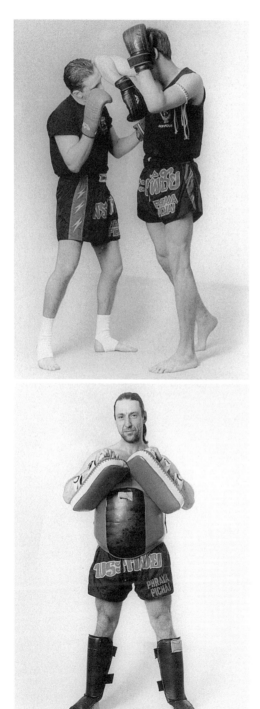

Fig. 91 The Spinning Elbow always strikes down and onto the opponent.

TOP LEFT: Fig. 90 Make sure that the guard is kept high as you move in to strike the opponent.

LEFT: Fig. 92 Tony is wearing the equipment normally used in Muay Thai training.

tinues to turn and drop the elbow in a downward strike to the crown of the opponent's head.

Once you have understood and practised the strikes and footwork it will be time to put them into practice against pads and bags. Eventually you may use them in competition and become truly successful.

Equipment

Muay Thai more than any other martial art makes full use of pads and bags. Indeed without the traditional Thai Pads, Muay Thai would never have evolved to its current state. We can see the types of pads used in training and the sequential photos also show how the pads are used in a freestyle manner.

The Thai Long Pads are used for all types of techniques and must be held firmly with adequate resistance being placed against them as the boxer strikes them. Do not hold the pads in a light manner. The padman and the boxer could get injured! The padman may also use the belly shield in conjunction with the long pads and this will allow the boxer to practise his front kicks, knees and clinchwork in a more improvised fashion. In its ultimate form, the padman will also wear the heavy shin pads and throw kicking techniques at the boxer. This is how he will learn to defend and counter-attack immediately. He will not practise pre-set drills but respond to the padman as if he were fighting him. This is the art of freestyle pads.

The heavy bag (*see* Fig. 103) is also used to great effect and does not require a partner. This makes it perfect for those that train alone. It serves two functions:

1. To work basic power techniques
2. To condition the boxer's weapons through repetitive practice.

Figs 93 & 94   Work the Freestyle Pads in a relaxed and fluid manner.

Fig. 95   Staying relaxed, Tony (left) absorbs Paul's Teep.

Any training regime always includes use of the heavy bag.

The uppercut bag has also been adopted from western boxing and is used for practice with the elbows.

Wrapping the Fists

Hand bindings have always been used in the art of boxing and Muay Thai is no exception. In fact Muay Thai has a history of binding the hands for combat that dates

Figs 96 & 97   Work the Freestyle
Pads in a relaxed and fluid manner.

Figs 98 & 99 Both the padman and the boxer stay focused and aware throughout.

Fig. 100 A good padman will interact with the boxer by launching attacks making the boxer defend and counter.

back to the late eighteenth century when exponents used hemp ropes, wrapped in such a way that they would inflict cuts and serious damage to the opponent. This method is called *Kad Cheug* and was discontinued after the death of a boxer at Lak Muang Stadium.

Kad Cheug would have knots woven into them and the bindings would reach up to the elbows. There are apocryphal stories about glue and glass being utilized but there is no documentary evidence to support these stories.

It is said that a boxer feels that his hands are like steel when well wrapped. This is no exaggeration and it is exactly what you should be trying to achieve. Modern-day methods of wrapping vary from camp to camp. However, what does remain the same are the rules that govern the sport of Muay Thai. The rule relating to wrappings is quite specific. They state that each binding must be made from a strip of cloth measuring at most 12yd (11m) in length by 2in (5cm) in width. Up to 6ft (1.8m) of adhesive tape may be used but must be put on the knuckles. When taping the hands, take your time paying particular attention to the tightness of the wrapping. Clench the fists periodically and check that you can still feel your fingers!

Fig. 101   Jim (padman) launches various attacks at the boxer, increasing the work rate as the rounds go by.

Nowadays the bindings are used for protection rather than destruction. It is to bind the hands in such a way as to prevent injury to the boxer. Support is needed for the eight carpals of the wrist joint, the five metacarpals of the hand and the thumb.

The sequence shown in Fig. 104 on pages 85 & 86 is a very basic one and is favoured in Thailand. Follow the sequence and good luck!

Other protective equipment would include the gumshield and of course a protective groin guard. Some fighters also prefer to wear ankle supports to give strength to the Achilles' tendon area.

Fig. 102 Here we see Tony block Jim's attack; he would counter-attack immediately.

Fig. 103 Any well-equipped gym will have heavy bags for training.

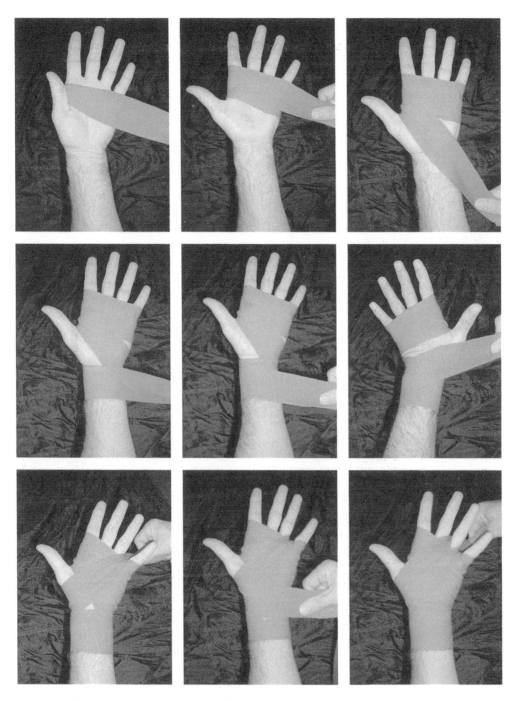

PAGES 85–6: Fig. 104   Binding the hands.

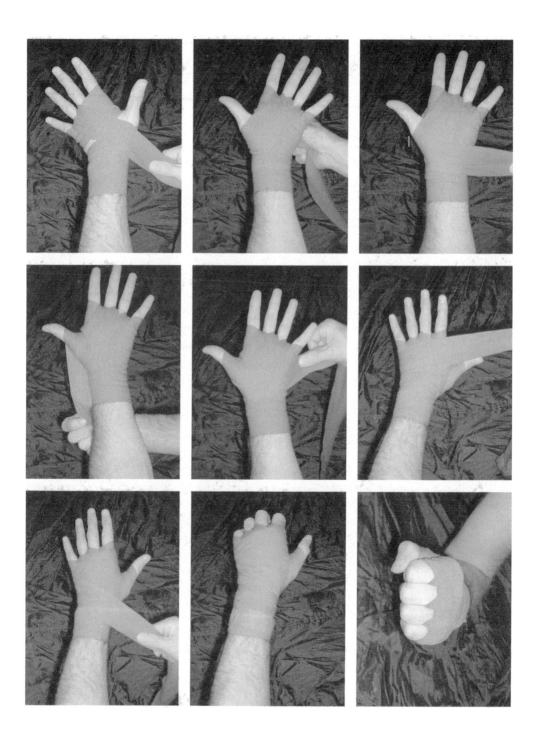

3 Clinchwork: Grappling Thai Style

When a western boxer is having problems or if he is getting tired what does he do? Aside from making a dash for it, he tends to lean on his opponent clinching the arms tightly around the opponent. The referee at this point steps in and pulls them apart. In Thailand this would never happen. Indeed it's partly because of this that we see Thai boxing as a brutal sport. We see the men clinching and the referee does nothing to stop it! The two boxers rain down elbows and knee attacks on one another as the referee stands by watching. Sometimes it can look messy and I have even heard western commentators exclaiming that this was the unco-ordinated part of Thai Boxing. Nothing however, could be further from the truth. This 'in fighting' or 'Clinchwork' is an art in itself and has been developed by the Thai into a very effective method of opponent control, providing the boxer understands the techniques involved. The boxer who masters this range masters the fight as the two fighters will invariably end up here anyway. In the street a fight can in some cases end up as a grappling match too! In Thailand it is practised regularly as part of the training programme and builds stamina and strength like no other exercise. Because it is close range it also prepares one psychologically for real combat.

Let's look at the technique in its most basic form. When two boxers fight they will work the long ranges with kicks and then start to move into punching range. If a boxer's hands are not particularly good the quick-thinking fighter will step into close-range through the hands where he will either execute powerful close-range attacks, such as elbow strikes, or he will simply grab hold of the opponent. When grabbing the opponent some teachers are of the opinion that the boxer should move the hips in toward the opponent quickly and tightly. You must do this in order to thwart any knee attacks the opponent may counter with, slipping one hand, then the other, behind the opponent's head. Note the hand position in the accompanying photograph. This will give superior control of the head allowing you to move the opponent around easily.

Mr Pimu of W.P.T. Gym in Bangkok currently teaches what I consider a far more powerful method that advocates the use of locking up the shoulders and keeping the neck and head tucked in.

This locks the opponent up, preventing them from getting your head down, thereby making you vulnerable to powerful attacks. The body should be arched at this point with a curved spine and you can now exert force down on your opponent's neck, controlling him down and into position for the knee attacks (see Fig. 105). In this position it is impossible for him to counter and you now have the upper hand taking the opponent up and into the ropes where you can thwart any evasion plan he may have had. The photo sequences show the types of drills Pimu uses (see Figs 109–111).

Fig. 105
Standard Clinch
position.

Pimu has also devised some superb strategies for dealing with this type of clinch too! It is possible at this stage of the game to pull the opponent's head onto your shoulder. This would serve to disorient the boxer making him vulnerable to quick movements of your hips that in turn, will twist him about opening up the mid-section to knee attacks. A great variety of knee attacks are used to maximum effect. Areas to concentrate on include the ribs, bladder, thigh, and even the head (*see*

Fig. 106 Stay high on the toes and raise the shoulders. Keep arms at right angles.

Fig. 107
Notice the
effect this has
on an
opponent.

Fig. 108   Exert force to the outside and pull the head down.

Fig. 108). Of course you must also remember that the opponent will be trying to get hold of your head, arms and even the body by moving from the outside to the inside position.

When slipping into the inside position it is imperative that it is done quickly and economically and that the hips are used as the driving force. Do not rely on the strength of the arms alone. This will tire you very quickly. The arms incidentally should be locked into a 90-degree position and should now be immovable.

It is this 'inside position' that the boxer looks for. It allows him to dominate the opponent. Gaining and keeping this position is all-important. If you control the head you control the man (*see* Figs

Fig. 109   As the Clinch is put on, defend by lifting your right arm ...

Fig. 110   ... then hold onto the arm with a Swan Neck Catch.

Fig. 111   Pulling the arm around and down, simultaneously driving the Knee into the midsection.

Fig. 112   As always the head is the main target!

Fig. 113 Phil (left) has the 'inside position'.

Fig. 114 Pulling Phil's neck with his right hand, Bob is able to slip the left ...

Fig. 115   ... and then the right hand into the 'inside position' thus taking control.

109–112). This is a basic principle of combat, to control the head both physically and psychologically. When we control physically we can disturb the equilibrium of the opponent and then either throw them to the ground or attack with elbows and knees. It is impossible to show in pictures the 'feel' of the Clinchwork and the dynamic interchange of energy required. All we can do is give a brief hint of the position of the body during the separate phases. One of the phases is the Clinch Release. This is simply a series of methods used by the fighter to release himself from the grip of a really strong fighter or elaborate locks and twists of the body can release the strongest opponent and open him up to an elbow or knee attack. The hips, as always, need to be used with power to hold the inside position and a constant movement around the ring will be seen. At times you may upset the balance of your opponent. Use this as an opportunity to throw him to the ground and, as well as gaining you a point, it will demoralize him. As this is a sporting aspect of Muay Thai, it is not permitted to trip up, reap or hip-throw the opponent. These are however not to be neglected in a street situation. The principle of using 4oz to move 4,000lb applies here. Let the opponent do the work for you. Keep relaxed and go with the flow.

Fig. 116   From the guard position Paul (right) ...

Fig. 117   ... catches Woz's neck. Woz reaches around catching Paul with his left hand and right hand in the crook of the arm.

Fig. 118   Taking the initiative Woz pulls Paul and reaches through ...

Fig. 119   ... to the 'inside position', ...

Fig. 120 ... turning Paul quickly to the left ...

Fig. 121 ... and finishing with a Forward Knee to the body.

Fig. 122   There are a of variety of clinch releases, one handed …

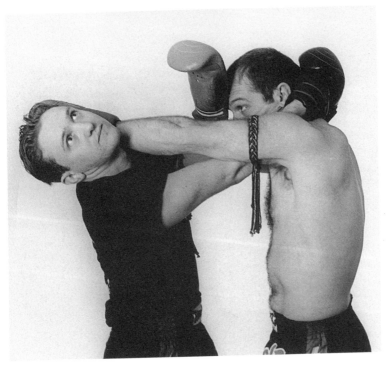

Fig. 123   … with a push or a twist …

Fig. 124　… and sometimes a lock.

Fig. 125　A two-handed push is also effective …

Fig. 126   ... but always finishing with a knee.

Shaking the opponent with rapid jerks of the arms and body will unnerve and release an opponent. Obviously the most skilful and efficient way is to use the footwork and hip-twist, pulling the opponent this way then another. Using your footwork is vital. Sometimes, in the initial stages of the clinch, you should also attempt to take control of the arms. One of the best ways is to lift the shoulder as the incoming grab approaches and simply twist your body into the arm. This locks his arm against yours and makes it impossible for him to counter (*see* Fig. 129). Unnerving an opponent is vitally important. To be thrown to the ground at ease by an opponent is a humiliating experience and one that should be avoided.

Fig. 127   A pulling and pushing action can also be effective ...

Fig. 128 ... as can a simple push.

BELOW: Fig. 129 Here, Bob simply lifts his left shoulder, twisting his body and effectively trapping Phil's arm.

Fig. 130   A well-placed Neb or Peck Kick stamped out will often break a good clinch.

Psychologically it has a disabling effect on all but the strongest fighters. Never neglect kicks in the clinch. If the opponent moves back, a well-placed peck kick or stamp will go some way to helping you take control of the fight (*see* Fig. 130). Some of the Clinchwork and throwing techniques we practise at the Phraya Pichai Camp in Birmingham involve throwing the opponent at sharp objects and moving objects. This is only done in the context of self-protection, it is not recommended in the ring!! Clinchwork is a much maligned and misunderstood art and I hope that this chapter goes in some way to improve matters.

4 Combination Techniques

Pre-set combinations most commonly used in training are as follows and can all be done on the bag or, with the help of a partner, on the pads. Always start off developing your technique rather than speed or power. This is the best way to train and reaps the greatest benefits.

JAB, CROSS, LEFT HOOK

JAB, CROSS, LEFT UPPERCUT

JAB, LEFT SAWK, RIGHT CROSS

LEFT TEEP, JAB, RIGHT CROSS, RIGHT DTAE TO LEG

LEFT TEEP, RIGHT DTAE LOW, LEFT KOW

Fig. 131   Champion Peter Hefford works combinations in a fighters' class on the Long Pads.

LEFT TEEP, SKIP LEFT DTAE MID-LEVEL, JAB, RIGHT CROSS

LEFT TEEP, RIGHT TEEP, RIGHT SAWK, CLINCH AND TURN

DOUBLE FORWARD KOW (in the clinch), TURN, PUSH AWAY, LEFT TEEP

CLINCH, KOW, TURN, SKIP LEFT KOW, RIGHT KOW, TURN, REPEAT KNEES

LOW DTAE, HIGH DTAE (EITHER LEGS), TEEP

LEFT JAB, RIGHT DTAE (MID-LEVEL), RIGHT KOW, RIGHT DTAE × 2

JAB, RIGHT CROSS, RIGHT HOOK, OUTSIDE CLINCH, SIDE KNEE × 2

LEFT TEEP, STEP IN LEFT SAWK, RIGHT SAWK

DOUBLE JAB, FEINT RIGHT CROSS, DTAE (MIDDLE LEVEL)

LEFT SHIN BLOCK, RIGHT MID-LEVEL DTAE, JAB, RIGHT CROSS, LEFT UPPERCUT

CROSS BLOCK, LEFT TEEP, LEFT JAB, RIGHT HOOK, CLINCH, KOW × 2

There are many more combinations available to the boxer. Use your imagination but don't get stuck in the trap of slavishly following set drills or training for the ring by set patterns. A fight is a constantly evolving and therefore changing entity. Know your basics, determine the weakness of your opponent and deal with the fight by adaptation. Remember: *stick to the basics*. Many famous fighters have built their reputation on just one technique!

5 Ringcraft

Running Rings around the Opponent

Competitive Muay Thai is about one thing and one thing only. Winning the fight! Taking second place to that maxim is to be able to hit the opponent without being hit oneself. It's as simple as that. However, there are many boxers about (and this I address to their coaches) who hope this will happen by good luck rather than good management. It doesn't happen like that if your opponent has superior technique, stamina and *ringcraft*.

If you have never fought in the ring it can be one of the scariest things you will ever do. This is because it is physical

Fig. 132 A typical training ring.

confrontation in an enclosed space where the fighter has no chance of escape. If you are not aware of the possibilities and positive aspects of fighting in the ring, you will become so with the guidance of a good coach. Traditionally, the competition ring is 22sq ft and a training ring is usually 16sq ft. Training in this way allows you a greater feeling of freedom when you do go into competition. When sparring in the ring take the fight to the opponent by being the first to the centre of the ring and the first to move in on the opponent. You gain a psychological and physical advantage in the initial stages of the fight. This approach has many positive aspects. The opponent is immediately taken by surprise and as well as being physically threatened is psychologically shaken too. If the boxer continues to maintain authority by keeping up this pattern of behaviour, he now has only his fitness and technical ability to worry about.

Ringcraft is all about creating openings and scoring is about taking advantage of these openings. An essential part of training and fighting in the ring is the ability of the fighter to take control. Taking control is generally dictated by three things; Rhythm, Planning, and Form. Each boxer has his own rhythm, a basic rhythm of work that will dictate his style. This is also dictated by his level of fitness. If a boxer understands this principle he can set up a rhythm with his opponent, break it, and then pick out the openings in his defence. It is then up to the boxer to exploit these areas of weakness and take control. Each fighter has a plan of campaign. Even the most hopeless of boxers has a basic idea of what they want to achieve. This is based upon the boxer's build, style, fitness and temperament. The successful boxer is one who can adapt his plans to suit the fight. All competition has a form or movement pattern. This involves the relative positions and movement of the fighters around the ring. Control of this space is the foundation of winning. Dominating the centre, cutting the opponent off at the angles, lateral movement with angular attacks and constant changes of direction all serve to upset the opponent's tactics, plans and rhythms. The fighter will also make use of a technique known as Feinting.

Feinting, by definition, is the technique of making an opponent think that you are about to make a move or deliver a specific strike; and then you do something else! Essentially the feint has three phases:

a. Feint
b. Counter response by the opponent
c. Your Attack (the counter to the counter)

Mind you, they don't always work so expect the unexpected. The opponent may be feigning surprise from your feint, in order to set you up for their attack. This is his feint! Sounds complicated? It can be! Another aspect of feinting is the drawing in of the opponent. This usually means deliberately exposing a target and waiting for the attacker to come charging in. Careful consideration must be made of:

a. Distance
b. Confidence
c. Footwork

Obviously a and c are mutually inclusive and should be practised. Confidence is a behaviour that is developed through continual practice in the ring. An example of drawing would be to drop your lead hand, step across the incoming opponent with a low roundhouse that he may block, then counter his counter immediately with a right cross to the jaw.

Feints are done with

- Footwork – Sudden changes as in the replacement step.
- Kicks and Knees – Feint in one direction and then change legs or technique – for example, Front Kick to Roundhouse Kick.
- Hands and Elbows – Feign a Jab then change to close Elbow Strike with the same arm.
- Clinchwork – Pull in one direction and then suddenly change, turning a defensive move into an offensive one and even utilizing the ropes when in the clinch.

It is the job of the fighter to draw his opponent in, and feinting attacks do just that. When fighting, be unpredictable. Always keep your opponent wondering what is going to happen next. Constant movement of the feet and hands, the use of the replacement step, or even just standing still, all keep the opponent guessing. Once you set up this approach see how it affects your opponent. It's like a game of chess, just a little tougher! Learn also to 'trigger' your opponent's response and see how you can take advantage of any openings that that might create. What are his mannerisms? What is his style? Does he defend well?

Fig. 133 Sparring practice. Both fighters wear protective shin pads to prevent injuries in training.

Fig. 134 Sparring practice. Use the knee with care, lightly tapping it into the stomach area.

Fig. 135   Make good use of the elbows against blows to the body ...

Fig. 136   ... and then use them as weapons to the opponent's head.

Fig. 137   Paul defends against Bob's jab ...

What's his favourite method of attack? All of these are recognized by sparring in the gym. Note that in training fighters always wear protective gear such as shin pads to prevent injuries.

However, it is important to note that training in the gym is simply a preparation for the real thing. It is true to say that sparring in the gym has an air of predictability about it. Its atmosphere is safe

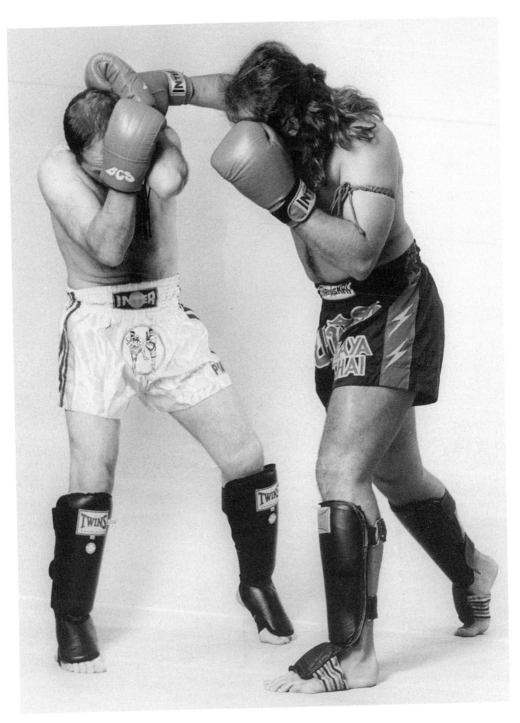

Fig. 138   ... and follows up with a right hook!

and secure. When you spar with familiar boxers you are already capable of exploiting their characteristics. You train with them enough to know how they behave. When you spar in competition and it's for real, it is quite different. Always spar with new people and strangers. Friendly competitions, between rival camps, are a great way of doing this. There is no pressure on you to win as there are no winners or losers. This keeps you on your toes and allows you to clear your mind of indecision and doubts. A clear mind will always be preferable to one cluttered by fears and doubts. Once perfected, ringcraft opens up a new world of possibilities in your sparring and you may even end up a champion!

In summary, then, I would like to leave you with a few tips.

Ringcraft hints:

- Have confidence in your abilities.
- Position of the head and eyes is vitally important in the clinch and when moving in on the opponent.
- Attacks should be varied constantly from upper body to legs.
- Always vary the angle of attack.
- Set up a rhythm and pattern then break it.
- Depth of stance is important for the generation of power from a feint.
- Be psychologically prepared as well as physically prepared.
- Finally, *you* must control the fight. Take the fight to the opponent.

Fig. 139   Scottish Champion Paul Stein holds up his arms in victory. The referee is Tony Myers, International Coach, Referee and Judge.

6 Coaching the Fighter

The Role of the Coach in Muay Thai

A coach can either make or break a fighter, in some cases even if the fighter has tremendous natural ability. Natural ability is an asset but not having confidence in that ability is almost as bad as not having it at all! So it is important that a coach understand his role in the development of the student and will embody these principles and pass them on through sound physical and psychological training methods to his student or fighter under his care. He must set an example for others to follow, not just in the way he conducts himself in the gym, but also in his everyday activities.

It is the coach's job to assess each individual fairly. He should aim to instill in the student self-confidence, the ability to concentrate on the task in hand and the ability to relax and enjoy the training they are

Fig. 140 Bob coaching a large group of fighters at the Phraya Pichai Camp HQ in Birmingham.

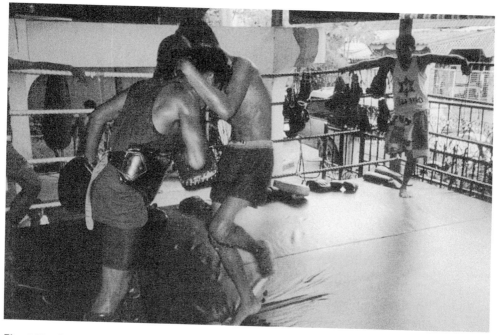

Fig. 141   Mr Pimu looks on as two boxers are put through their paces in his gym in Bangkok.

undergoing. Systematic training by the coach should help promote these qualities in the student. However, the coach should be aware that every student has his/her own wants and desires, and that although they may be highly motivated to achieve their goals, they still carry with them certain irrational fears. For some it may be the fear of failure, with others it may be the fear of success itself. Students are not as straightforward as some of the training manuals would have you believe. The underlying principle behind every aspect of Muay Thai is a balance between the physical and the psychological and it is the job of the coach to attempt to get to grips with all aspects of the student under his tuition – but within the appropriate boundaries of the coach–student relationship.

If a coach has to understand where his student is in terms of confidence then the coach himself must have confidence in his own ability to teach. Any doubts that may creep in will be picked up by the student and affect their performance in training. The coach should be positive and enthusiastic, giving equal training in the physical techniques (that enhance the student's ability to relax), and mental training that will prepare the student to handle the different levels of stress associated with competition. All fighters suffer from nerves; this is quite natural and should be accepted by the coach and the student and must be used in a positive way through encouragement and physical training. There are many books available on this aspect of training and all of them talk of support as the key to coping. The coach must give adequate support but without fostering dependence.

Diet and Rest

The demands that are placed on the body when a fighter is training for a competition are tremendous and, like a finely tuned racing engine requiring only the best fuel, so, too, must the fighter feed himself the right mix of foodstuffs to help him work out and aid his recovery from strenuous training sessions. It is important to balance the intake of carbohydrates, sugars and starches that provide the fighter with energy, with protein, calcium and vitamins to aid tissue regeneration. The coach should try to be aware of any nutritional deficiencies his student may have and should not put the student on any of the 'fad' diets that are being constantly promoted. A healthy balanced diet is what is required, keeping well clear of highly processed, fatty and sweet sugary foodstuffs.

It is very important for the fighter to find his correct competition weight. This should be a natural weight and not one forced upon the body in an attempt to fight in different weight categories. Weight loss, where necessary, should only be achieved through diet; sweating weight off a fighter achieves very little. The fighter is simply losing body liquid not fat and the practice of sweating some weight off prior to a fight is dangerous. There is the chance that this could dehydrate a boxer thus preventing him from delivering his best performance in the ring. It is the coach's job to decide on the competition weight of his fighter and to help the fighter achieve it through a monitored diet. Finally, a fighter should never compete on a full stomach. When under physical and psychological stress in the ring, the last thing a fighter wants is for his body to try and cope with digesting a large meal.

Adequate rest, before and after a fight, is also very important. It is up to the boxer to ensure that he has the right amount of sleep and rest before the fight. It is the coach's job to ensure that the fighter understands the principles of relaxation and to give a massage to the fighter at the end of a hard session, and just before and after his fight. It is advisable that the coach take a recognized massage course and not simply give the student a quick rub down.

Preparing for the Contest

A coach should have pride in his appearance. If the coach is untidy then it follows that the boxer too will be untidy. Always appear in good shape and wearing clean garments for a contest. The coach must also make sure that a fighter is aware of the rules, the reasons for the rules, and which rules are relevant to the particular situation. If everything is in its place the fighter will feel more secure.

The fighter, as well as understanding the rules of the contest must also be taught the significance of the rituals associated with Muay Thai and should be conversant with his camp's Ram Muay. These rituals must be respected and used in their correct context. The coach must not have a flippant attitude to these procedures as they can be used to great psychological effect with the student.

The coach must make sure that all equipment being used is clean and accounted for. A typical medical bag should contain the following items:

Beaker or spray bottle
Cotton Buds
Ice Pack or Gel Bag
Sponge in a plastic bag
Sterile gauze pads
Towel and hand towel

Fig. 142   World-class coach and mentor Pimu massages British fighter Ed prior to him winning his first fight at the famous Rajdamnern Stadium in Bangkok.

Medical supplies should include the following:

Scissors small and medium-size surgical type
Bandages of different sizes
Ananase
Varidase
Chymoral
Bonjela
Collodian
Eardrops
Elastoplast, assorted
Thai Oil
Eye drops
Nasal drops
Nobecutane spray
Savlon
Triangular sling bandage
Tweezers
Vaseline

Other equipment such as a stopwatch, coaching pads and long mitts should be taken along by the coach. The coach should also check out the ring to ensure it conforms to the standards laid down by both the Professional Thai Boxing Association and the International Muay Thai Association in Thailand. For example, is there an adequate warm-up area? Is there an area for massage? Are the boxers in a warm area?

The boxer, too, has a responsibility in terms of his appearance. Is he clean, are his toenails short? Does his gumshield fit snugly and is the groin protector secured? The coach will always check these items but it is important for the fighter also to have responsibility for them.

Finally

Every boxer has his own superstitions. Familiar patterns in behaviour develop that make the boxer feel secure and become part of the fighter's personal ritual. Do not ignore these seemingly irrational habits. These are powerful tools in helping your fighter focus on the task at hand.

A massage before the fight is very important as it assists in preparing the boxer's body for the fight. It should be done briskly and by someone qualified to do the job. What you musn't do is a slow massage to help him relax. The masseur should give an envigorating type of massage designed to get the muscle temperature up, giving the boxer energy. The massage over, the fighter is ready to have his hands taped to prevent injury. Many variations exist in the method of taping but basically the taping procedure must fully support the joints of the hand and wrist with just the right amount of tension. Tape and hand wraps must always be clean.

The fighter is now ready for the warm-up. This should happen in three phases:

1. Non-specific warm-up. This is where the fighter goes through his warm-up routine as practised in the gym, light skipping and joint rotations being the norm.

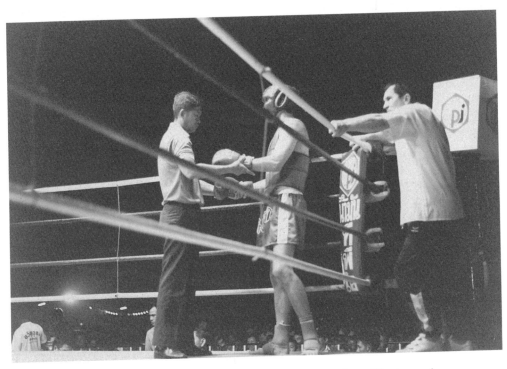

Fig. 143   The referee checks the fighter's gloves before the fight. The boxer is wearing a head guard and body protector as this is an amateur competition.

2. The specific warm-up. This should reflect the type of tactics to be used in the fight ahead and is usually performed as shadow boxing.
3. Main Body. Here the Long Pads are brought into use and combinations are practised preparing the boxer for the fight by instilling confidence and relaxation in his techniques. Many coaches prefer only the simplest warm-up. The Ram Muay!! They believe that it is counterproductive for the fighter to tire himself out in a strenuous warm-up prior to the fight. Far better to relax and watch the strengths and weaknesses of the other boxers as they expend energy warming up in the changing room!

With the warm-up completed, the boxer has the garland or good luck charms and a towel placed around his neck and the boxing gown is placed around him. The feet and hands are checked and gloves inspected and put on. Any excess oil must be wiped away from the body and finally the Mongkon is placed on the head and the boxer bows three times to the teacher. Everything has been done that can be done to ensure the boxer's success.

The Fight

The boxer has been inspected by the referee and can now perform his Wai Kru and Ram Muay. If the coach has done his job the fighter should now be ready to fight with confidence. During the bouts the coach will give words of encouragement, conducting himself in a positive manner, assessing the situation, his fighter's performance and his weaknesses and strengths. How effective are his tactics and techniques? The assistant coach, or second, should be keeping an eye on the time, informing the coach at regular intervals, in particular the last 10 seconds of the bout.

At the end of each round the gumshield is removed, any injuries must be attended to by the second, whilst the coach gives words of advice and support. Cuts are cleaned with fresh gauze before the application of an adrenalin pad. Pressure is required and this should be done by the second. Slight swellings or bruising may be rubbed and/or an ice pack applied. In the event of a nose bleed the nose is pinched and the head tilted forward. Finally the boxer is towelled down, his gumshield returned and the second and the coach leave the ring as 'seconds away' is called.

At the end of the match the boxers are led away to wind down with gentle stretching exercises; this is believed to help prevent stiffness the following day. The boxer must leave on the gown to retain body heat and any sign of injury must be treated following a shower.

If a contest is stopped, for example, in the event of a knockout or if the towel is thrown in, a doctor should be brought in to examine the boxer. If concussion is evident, then the boxer must be taken to a hospital immediately where he should undergo a thorough examination. Always accompany the boxer home in the event of concussion.

Analysis of the fight should be made at the next training session and not before. If a fighter has lost his fight he should be praised, told that he did his best with good technique and spirit. It is usual for a boxer who has lost a fight to learn far more than one who has won. Remember, however, that any criticism should be constructive and should help the boxer to see his weaknesses. It is the job of the coach to see a weakness, problem or loss as an opportunity to improve his fighter's abilities.

A good coach must also be critical of his own performance and abilities.

Fig. 144   A successful first-time win goes to Andy Howard standing next to his coach Bob who is flanked by his corner men Marcus Bailey and Steve Mcarron.

Was the fighter prepared both psychologically and physically?

Was the fighter motivated?

Was the boxer on schedule for the fight and was the training programme the right one?

If a coach can be self-critical he will go on to be a superior coach with a long list of successful, highly motivated fighters.

7 Judging Muay Thai

In this chapter I propose to spend some time looking at a topic that concerns me greatly. It is an area that is fraught with misinterpretation and simple misunderstandings. For the Thai boxer in the UK it seems at once confusing and annoying. For the spectator, too, there is confusion and ignorance and in the case of the many Thai Boxing competitions I have witnessed it occurs all too often. Bad judging and refereeing. It stems mainly from the fact that what we practise in the UK is not Muay Thai but many forms of Thai Kickboxing with different rules for different competitions. No wonder we are confused! How can we sort it out?

The judge and the referee play an important role in the function of the fight. If strict and universally accepted guidelines and rules are not understood and adhered to then the result can often be unfair and infuriating. However, we need to look at the fighters and their coaches first. What is their role in all of this? Obviously if a fighter is unaware of the rules of a particular style of fighting then he really doesn't stand a chance. The coach should make sure his boxer is fully aware of the conditions and rules to be used. This is especially confusing because of the different organizations that exist in this country. In Muay Thai there should be no such confusion. Straightforward rules have been used in Thailand since after the Second World War and are used effectively and (usually) without bias in the major stadiums of Bangkok.

In the UK however, it starts to go horribly wrong. Because so few (so-called) Thai Boxing Groups seem to follow these rules we tend to end up with fighters unaware of the implications of the techniques they are using. This is solely the responsibility of the officials and the instructors within the sport. I, for one, thought I knew, more or less, what refereeing and judging were all about. The courses on judging and refereeing I had attended within the BTBC had me well prepared. However, once I had attended the course for judges and referees in Uttaradit (Northern Thailand), I realized how many gaps there were in my knowledge. I heard the words of Tony Moore echoing in my head: 'There's not much real Muay Thai in the UK.' He was right. What I saw was what he had spoken about time after time on the courses he runs. Obviously the Thai had been doing it a long time and really had the whole thing sussed. Weren't we doing Muay Thai here in the west?

The answer is quite simply 'no'. Some Muay Thai can be seen but most of it is still carrying with it the remains of a hybrid system that places more value on the use of boxing than it does on the use of the knee, the kicks, the elbows and the clinch. (This never happens in Thailand.) The knee, although a simple weapon, is still used very badly and many judges really haven't a clue when it comes to scoring it. Another technique, often badly practised and not at all understood by the judges, coaches or fighters is Clinchwork. What we should see is the skilful use and control of bodyweight. Subtle twisting and turning of the opponent and the subsequent entry of the knee to the opponent's body. For my money go and watch one of Will Hastings' (Pra Chao Suaa Camp) fights. Now, he knows how to use the Clinch and the Knee. Mind you he does train under Tony Myers, one of the most knowledgeable Muay Thai coaches in Europe. His boys spend time looking at what the Thai are doing, applying it and then putting it into practice.

When it comes to kicks we Brits are still way behind the Thai. Some of the fighters I have seen still flick the kicks out of range and hope to score the points. The kick Teep (Front Kick) or Dtae (Round Kick) has to make good contact with the opponent. In the case of the Teep it's the ball of the foot and with the Dtae, the shin area, the best targets being first the head and secondly the body. This applies to the Kow (Knee) and of course Sawk (Elbow) too. Hands score much less than these techniques and are way down the hierarchy. If a fighter is thrown to the canvas this, too, is a high scoring technique and if the fighter's leg is caught cleanly and held, this raises the fighter's score as it is deemed superior in a technical sense.

Even with this information we still need to know what we are looking at in terms of technique.

Fig. 145   A good judge stays focused and calm.

Briefly, the requisites of a good Kow or Knee is good distance. There is no value in having a beautiful technique that is powerful and fast if it misses the target. It is the coach's job to teach this and the judge's job to look for it. Hips should be thrust toward the opponent adding power and penetration to the weapon. The fighter should also have the arms in a good defensive position and the point of the knee should strike the target. It must be quick and relaxed and the fighter should be up on the toes when delivering it. Finally the fighter should show control of the Knee when he retracts it or places it down for the next technique. All of these criteria would constitute superior technique. Anything short of this – that is, not coming high onto the toes, would be deemed good. If three or four of the above criteria were missing, then poor technique is obviously being displayed. With Dtae (Round Kick) the same criteria would apply. Good distance, good timing, hitting the target in an arc, hitting with the shin, pivoting on the ball of the foot, being relaxed but quick and a defensive arm position are all important points to look for when judging and teaching the fighter. I could go on in great detail but all of this is being taught on a regular basis within the TIBC so that the UK has Muay Thai fighters we can be proud of in the International arena.

To sum up briefly, it is the job of the judge to determine who was the most effective contestant in terms of:

a. Controlling the action
b. Causing the most disadvantage to the opponent through the use of the full repertoire of techniques
c. The effectiveness of the strikes, their accuracy and technical quality
d. The defensive abilities of the contestants.

It is not possible through the publication of a book to do justice to the task of educating the west as to what real Muay Thai is. Let's just say that there is not much about and the public are losing out by seeing a poor relation that we dare to call Thai Boxing in this country. If you want to see Real Muay Thai I'm afraid you need to save up and travel to Thailand.

8 The Three-Month Training Regime

Let's make one thing clear. Training in the UK is very different from training in Thailand. A typical day in the life of a Thai Boxer in Bangkok starts at 6am with a 7–10 km (4–6 mile) run followed by training until about 10am. The boxer then eats and rests until about 3pm when it all starts again. The training will consist of footwork, skipping, heavy bag-work, pad-work, clinch-work and sparring. This happens six days a week! In Thailand this is a job and is done out of economic necessity. In the UK it's just not that serious. We train for a variety of reasons and only a few students will end up fighting in the ring. Most students will be training for fitness and self-protection and a training regime should reflect that. Each session should take 1½ to 2 hours and be done only three days a week. If you intend competing then your training should reflect this and you should be running every day for at least 7 km (4½ mile).

Remember: Before commencing any form of physical training, speak to your doctor and if in doubt have a complete medical examination.

Your first session should be easy and the structure of the lesson plans should reflect this in that it gradually builds as does your appreciation of technique.

Each training session must be preceded by an adequate warm up period of at least 15 min. This will comprise skipping for at least three × 3 min rounds as well as general callisthenics. The body now warmed up, it is time to practise the basic footwork

drills explained in the earlier chapter. Practise these every day until they feel natural. In Thailand the fighters constantly practise their 'walking ' drills. Practise both left and right stances, and alternate them frequently

Footwork will be practised at every session for at least 10 min. After a few weeks combine these techniques with footwork in a relaxed and mobile fashion. This is known as Shadow Boxing. Do it at every session for at least 10 min before moving onto the pads and heavy bags. The remainder of the session will then be taken up with developing your sparring skills and Clinchwork Techniques.

Week 1/Week 2
Yaang Saam Khum 20min
Skipping 10min
Calisthenics 10 min (see ST table at end of chapter)
Shadow boxing 3 × 3min rounds
Heavy Bag work 3 × 3min rounds
Familiarization with footwork and basic punches and kicks
Combinations on the pads and/or bag:
Jab, Right Cross
Jab, Right Cross, Left Hook
Front Kick (Lead Leg)
Low Roundhouse Kicks (Right Leg)

Week 3/Week 4
Yaang Saam Khum 20 min
Skipping 3 × 3min
Calisthenics

Shadow Boxing 5 × 2min
Bag work:
   1st Round: Boxing 3min
   2nd Round: Boxing and Kicks
   3rd Round: Knees and Clinch

All rounds to last 3min with 1min rest between.

Combinations as previous weeks but also include uppercuts, forward knees, side elbows and peck kicks.

Week 5/Week 6

Yaang Saam Khum 20min
Skipping 4 × 3min
Shadow Boxing 5 × 2min

Review *all* boxing and elbow techniques together on pads and/or the heavy bag. Devote at least 30 min to this.

Review *all* kicking techniques in conjunction with Knees for 30min on pads and/or heavy bag.

Week 7/Week 8

Yaang Saam Khum 15min
Skipping 5 × 3min
Shadow Boxing 5 × 3min
Clinchwork (if partner available) 2 × 2min rounds
Combination techniques on heavy bag or pads to include *all* Kicks, Knees, Punches and Elbows studied so far, 5 × 3min rounds

Week 9

Rest Week

Weeks 10, 11 and 12

It is the final part of the three-month programme and you must now identify your weak points. Practise skipping and shadow boxing as normal, concentrating all of your attention on areas of training where you feel weakest.

You are now well on the road to becoming a Nak Muay (Thai Boxer).

Below is an outline of a simple Strength and Stamina Test that we use to assess the fitness levels of our students in the Camp.

If you have never trained before start at Level E.

The Stregnth/Stamina Test (ST)
Completion time for Level A & B should be around 3½ min

Exercise Level	A	B	C	D	E
Press-ups	30	25	15	10	5
Split Squats	30	25	15	10	5
Burpees	12	10	8	6	4
Crunches	30	25	15	10	8
Press-ups Close grip	15	10	6	4	3
Tuck Jumps	30	25	15	10	5
Scoops	20	15	10	8	6
Crossover Sit-ups	30	25	15	10	8

This test is designed to give an overall picture of endurance, stamina, strength and recovery rate. As students progress through the ranks they should refer back to the previous ST test to give an indication of their improvement.

9 Self Protection

The whole area of self protection is one that is beset with problems from the start. The law states that only 'reasonable force' may be used when defending oneself and we should be aware of this when protecting ourselves from the numerous muggers, criminals and opportunist attackers that walk the streets. Any system of self protection is only as effective as the person who uses it. If that individual is prepared both mentally and physically, then the outcome of any confrontation is likely to be in favour of that person. There are many martial arts that will develop physical mastery over the techniques of self-defence, but few teach any real methods of psychological and communication training. This is when it becomes self protection. It is these areas that are often neglected when a so-called 'trained' martial artist is injured by someone who has had no formal training at all.

The physical, psychological and communications skills needed for effective self protection are interdependent and should be taught alongside each other in any class curriculum.

It has been my experience that the only way to teach these techniques is through the implementation of a nine-point system I call SADSUPSCAS.

SADSUPSCAS is an acronym for the following nine principles of effective self protection and are as follows:

- Surprise
- Awareness
- Decisiveness
- Stay upright
- Physical training
- Speed
- Control
- Aggressiveness
- Simplicity

To demonstrate the interdependence of these principles, I will now provide an example.

You are walking down a dimly lit lane in an area that you suspect has a reputation for trouble. Muggings and attacks have taken place recently and normally you wouldn't venture through such a place. Tonight you have no choice. Realizing this is such a high risk area you maintain a high level of *awareness*. Using your senses you watch for anything suspicious, taking the various elements of your environment and the people in that environment. You listen intently for any strange noises, getting a feeling for the area you are walking through. Most people in this situation would now start to internalize their experience and start to worry about what could happen. You must not do this! To maintain a high level of awareness requires that you stay outside of your thoughts and only deal with what is happening in the real world, not the world you create inside your mind. You look around. Could you make good an escape if you ran? What is the terrain like? Are there street lights? Do you know your escape routes? If you must fight a

130

there any weapons at hand that you could use to defend yourself with? If you are attacked by an armed assailant a rolled up magazine can be used to jab at the opponent.

Two figures approach you and they don't look like they're going to ask you if you have the time. In fact they look like the sort of guys who would take your watch! You are now in a high state of alertness and the adrenalin buzz of fear sings in your ears. You must maintain *control*. You slow down your breathing and direct this nervous energy to your centre. This allows you to concentrate on the task at hand and helps give you a confident posture. It is true to say that this in itself can dissuade a potential attacker from the start. If you have trained well and rehearsed these scenarios, you will act with confidence and a sense of control. This act will change your physiological responses to the situation, preparing you for the confrontation well in advance. When it comes to protecting oneself, one must act within the law at all times. If you have the opportunity to talk to the potential aggressors then do so. Keeping your distance by verbal communication and control of your physical space is the first stage of self protection and takes place when you have the time. It is often the case that if the aggressors think that you have the edge over them by controlling the situation, they will turn their attention to a weaker target. Indeed, if you walk with a confident stride and appear to be aware, then it is highly unlikely that you will be threatened. It has been proven through research that opportunity muggers tend to go for those who appear weak and unaware of their surroundings.

One of them moves toward you aggressively, his body language displaying all the signs of potential attack. At this point, the law encourages you to diffuse the situation by either making good your escape as quickly as possible, or by handing over your watch. If neither of these options is possible you must act *decisively*. Your response must be *aggressive*. In other words, move forwards and in towards the attacker. The law states that you can attack pre-emptively if you feel that your physical well-being is threatened, but you must only attack with the level of force that is commensurate with the threat. In other words, if they appear unarmed then you are not, by law, allowed to attack them with a weapon. In this situation you would use a simple open-hand technique to the jaw or head, stopping the attacker with minimum force. If you have been serious in your *physical training* then you will defend yourself with *speed* which will surprise the assailants. *Surprise* is on your side in this situation. A direct attack is not what an assailant expects: use it to your advantage. The fight will be over very quickly if you act effectively but always *stay upright*. Do not to go to the ground with someone unless your grappling skills are as good as your hand and leg skills.

The above represents a very simplistic scenario of what occurs when a trained person is attacked. In order to understand each principle fully, more detailed explanations follow. The attack should be kept *simple*. A palm heel strike to the jaw, chin or forehead can often be enough to render an attacker stunned. If there are two or more attackers you may need to use an elbow or knee. Whatever you do, keep the techniques you use down to a minimum.

Having briefly looked at these principles let us take them one by one for a more detailed explanation.

Surprise

This is the first principle of effective self

Fig. 146 Bob 'lines up' the potential aggressor, maintaining control through distance.

Fig. 147 As the aggressor moves forward a well-aimed palm heel strike is delivered ...

protection. The element of surprise is yours to take and is related to two other principles:

Awareness – never let yourself be taken by surprise

Aggression – Do what is least expected of you

In a training situation with a partner, suddenly change your approach, surprise them and observe the reaction. A shout will surprise and give you valuable time to attack if this is necessary. Experiment in training with these techniques. Remember you must practise psychological techniques as much as the physical techniques of Muay Thai. Use your brain to create change, seeing and feeling yourself in the scenario winning the fight. If you can have a strong enough idea and belief, you will create the outcome you desire by changing your behaviour.

Fig. 148   ... dropping the opponent who is then finished off with an elbow strike.

Aggression

Do not be half-hearted in your response if the attack warrants it. If the attacker is armed, you will have to respond with attacks to soft areas of the body such as the groin. Under stress most people react with fear. Through training you will turn fear into aggression. This can be done by thinking of times in your life when you have done something without fear. When you have displayed these qualities of confidence in a given situation. Remember your driving test? Maybe you can remember your exams? The situation frightened you but you did it any way. This means that your brain knows how to use confidence as a technique. It knows how to deal with fear. If it can do it in one situation, it can be repeated again in a different context. It's the same as fear. It's simply something the brain has learned to do. It is a pattern of behaviour we can learn to change for certain situations.

For example, think of a time when you were totally confident. See what you saw, hear what you heard and feel what you felt. Go back to that time and relive it and see how good it makes you feel. Now double the feeling. You can feel this good whenever you want and not be a slave to other ideas and thoughts. If you get a clear picture in your mind's eye, look at it. How big is it? Is it in colour or black-and-white? Is it close or far away? Are you in the picture or can you see as though looking out of your eyes into the picture? Is it moving or still? These are known as submodalities in the area of behaviourial change work known as Neuro Linguistic Programming (NLP). Do the same with sound. Listen for tonal qualities. Does the sound seem loud or quiet? Is it more in one ear than the other? Where does it emanate from? Sometimes simply changing the sound can change the way you feel. Do you find you talk to yourself in a dismal tonality? Change the tonality, change the voice. Change a negative voice to one that sounds like your favourite cartoon character. I could never take the voice of Homer Simpson seriously. Could you? The same can be done with feelings. Where are they? In the torso, the arms, the head? Is it a warm feeling or cool? Does it pulse or hang? Is it heavy or light? Make a list of them and go into as much detail as possible with each of these submodalities. The more information you have, the better.

Now do the same with fear. Think of the last time you were in a confrontational situation. Go back in your mind's eye to that time and relive it. Notice the pictures, the feelings and the sounds. You can even recall, mentally, smells and tastes. After all, we experience the world through five senses, so get a really good representation. Now compare your submodalities for fear with those of confidence. Notice the differences? It is the difference that makes the difference. Now change those differences in the fear state to those of confidence and notice how it changes the way you feel. It is different isn't it? If the mental image of confidence is in the middle distance and that of fear is close up, move it away and notice how you feel. Sometimes people will say they need more distance on their problems. If this is the case then actually do that with your mental images. Take what they say literally! I use these techniques in many areas of my work, not just in the martial arts. Using these techniques soon becomes second nature and now your brain has learned how to deal with fear in a different way. In fact, you could train yourself to develop a mental habit that will allow you to 'switch on' an aggressive attitude. You are trained to deal with this. You are highly trained and motivated. The aggressor is usually neither.

Decisiveness

You must have the ability to act immediately and in the correct fashion. If you truly understand the principles of your art you will be on auto-pilot and respond in the correct way. This understanding only comes through dedicated training and constant repetition; working with your partner on simple, effective techniques. Again, visualization will play an important part in this process. The nervous system regards vividly imagined experience (a visualization) as actual experience. Through training you will be pre-setting natural responses. After all you won't have the time to consider your next move in a real situation.

Stay Upright

Maintain an upright and balanced posture at all times. Go to the ground only if it is to your advantage. For example, if someone is shooting at you! If you should end up being grabbed, use the principles of clinch-work, control the head of the attacker and, using twists and turns, disorient them. If they attempt to hit you this would be the time to use your natural weapons.

Physical Training

The old adage 'Survival of the Fittest' certainly holds true in the field of self protection. I would stress that body conditioning, stamina, speed and power take precedence over the desire to learn a great number of techniques.

Essentials of fitness can be summed up as the 'Five S Factor':

Stamina. Endurance or staying power. This can only be developed by placing stress on the cardiovascular system (heart and lungs). Aerobic exercises should be used as the foundation for building your fitness. Aerobic activity may be classified as that which involves exercises designed for steady and regular application of stress to the cardiovascular system. Examples are running, skipping, swimming and circuit training. Work on the heavy bag or focus pads as these would also suffice if practised correctly.

Speed. To improve speed, heavy pressure training such as punching the heavy bag at a high rate would be recommended. When training for speed, anaerobic training is generally used. Anaerobic activity is that which places exceptional stress on the cardiovascular system, so much so that the body is at its optimum level without a renewed supply of oxygen. A good example of this would be sprinting. It should also be mentioned that footwork improves your speed.

Strength. Here we are paying attention to the skeletal muscles of the body. Weight training is the ultimate type of exercise to practise in order to promote strength. However, training on the heavy bag should be structured to meet these needs.

Suppleness. The exercises and calisthenics that are used in this book will provide you with all the methods necessary to help you develop flexibility, mobility and agility in the body: all the components required to develop a superior combat-oriented physique.

Skill. All work relating to techniques, with or without a partner, with or without equipment. The acquisition of skill in techniques and the transfer of these into a self-protection situation is of primary importance. The ability to react with a reflex response incorporating SADSUPSCAS is the essence of skill. Your training must be geared to balance

Fig. 149   Bob steps inside a 'haymaker' punch driving his left elbow ...

Fig. 150 ... then his right into the attacker's head ...

Fig. 151   ... which is then grabbed and the opponent is then spun around ...

Fig. 152   ... and down ...

Fig. 153 ... onto the ground.

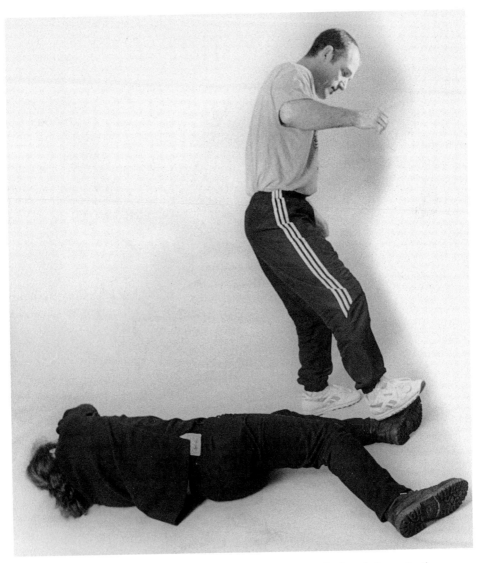

Fig. 154   If the opponent is armed, finish him off with a well-aimed stamp to the ankle to prevent further attacks.

the whole. Skill in technique will automatically provide you with power and speed.

The above is simply a guideline. Read as much as you can on this subject and develop your own workout patterns. When beginning training always set time aside to warm up the body otherwise strains and injuries will prevent you from training effectively if at all. Always motivate yourself to put 100 per cent into your workouts, be it conditioning or the learning of new techniques.

Speed

Your response to an attack must come quickly and take your assailant by surprise. The four requisites for a fast counter-attack are coordination, timing, distance and the ability to launch an attack without telegraphing it. All of these are encompassed in the practice of footwork. Effective footwork means you probably won't be there to be hit!

Control

No matter how technically proficient you are, if you lose self control and panic under the stress of an assault you will more than likely freeze and lose control of the situation. You are then at the mercy of your attacker. You must motivate your mental attitude. The psychological approach to training must be thorough. Accept that loss of control takes place in the absence of correct training, and that it is possible to eliminate this failing through regular training. There is also the control you must have over your opponent. This can only be accomplished by training yourself to move in on an attack, rather than away, and be aware of the degree of force required in a given situation. Whether you move in on a straight line to his centre, or working the angles at 45 degrees to the attack, the emphasis must always be to move in and neutralize, and ultimately control your attacker.

Awareness

Always maintain a high level of awareness when a situation seems to be developing. Never allow yourself to be taken by surprise. Be vigilant, aware of your environment, paying particular attention to anything or anyone who looks suspicious. Is the terrain rough or flat? Could you run?

Are there any obstacles? Is there room to manoeuvre if attacked? Are there any weapons to hand? Is there anything behind you right or left? Above or below? When training, practise awareness of your surroundings and the people training with you. Focus on your partner, but allow peripheral vision to take in any movements around.

The best fighter is the one who avoids trouble by being aware of their environment and their place in it, and thereby avoiding the situation by getting away from it.

Simplicity

Always keep your defence and subsequent counter-attack as simple as possible. Avoid kicking to the head when a kick to the groin would suffice. Avoid blocking an attack when evasion is more economical in terms of both strength and speed.

In conclusion, I consider the above principles essential to any form of effective self protection. They are universal and have worked for me and my students in many situations. As your training develops you will see changes happening in your life overall. Read between the lines and you will see a little more. It is this 'extra' ingredient that will separate you from the run-of-the mill martial artist.

The OODA Loop

This is quite simply an information-processing loop that is happening continuously no matter what you are doing. OODA is an acronym for:

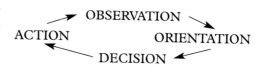

It is widely used throughout the Special Forces as an information-processing tool and is useful in helping you recognize the build-up that leads to a confrontational situation. Once recognized, you can act before they do. Essentially, we need to be constantly aware. We do this through observation. If something seems out of place we orientate, putting ourselves in the best possible position to gain the advantage. If this means you can run, then that is what you must do. You can only stand and fight if you have to. Fighting must be your last resort. We make the decision to do this and then act! Once we have acted we immediately return to observation and the cycle goes around again. Bear in mind that the assailant is also doing this unconsciously. By having a conscious awareness of these states, we are the ones in control. This is how we beat them. It is 'fighting without fighting'. Our job is to recognize his position in the sequence and act (hit or run) before he reaches his decision point. It is that simple.

Make a decision before they do.

10 Goal Setting: the Secret to Success

In order to achieve optimum performance in Muay Thai, whether it be for competition or self protection, it is necessary to train hard and train smart. In order to train hard it is necessary to have the desire to do well – that is, to come out on top and be a highly motivated individual. To train smart means not to waste time and energy moving in the wrong direction. In other words, to maintain your focus and achieve your desired outcomes.

If you are travelling somewhere it is necessary (if you wish to arrive on time) to plan the best possible route, working it out a stage at a time and then checking everything is in order before embarking. You will then have a plan of how to get there! You will inevitably arrive at the desired location.

It's no different if your journey is going to take you to a world title or being able to protect yourself on the street. If you don't plan the route, you're not going to get there. It's as simple as that. In fact every day you should plan to feel good about yourself and everything you do! It is a fact that if you feel good you will make better decisions about everything you are involved in. We can all spend time feeling bad and that also takes adequate planning! Feel good – make good decisions. Feel bad – make bad decisions. The choice is yours.

To plan for success in any venture requires a four-point plan:

1. Goals: Know what you want. Always frame them in a positive way ... and be specific about them.
2. Feedback: Know when you have got what you want and if you haven't then change your approach until you have.
3. Rewards: When you have it, does it make you feel good? Does it make others feel good?
4. Resources: Know what your resources are and where you can find them. If you feel that you do not have them, act as if you have!

Goals

In the early days of your training, you should sit down and write a list of the things you intend to achieve within the next month. Then see yourself achieving them in your mind's eye, feel them taking effect in your body, hearing the sounds that might be associated with these feelings. Use all of your senses when you think of a goal. You may even smell or taste something. We've all heard of the sweet smell of success. Maybe there is something in that statement.

Visualization has been used for years in sport, and is useful in helping you achieve goals; but the human organism experiences the world through five senses. If we tie ourselves to just one (visualization) we will be short-changing ourselves when it comes to personal development! When you plan your short-term goals *see* yourself achieving them, notice any *sounds*, *smells* or *tastes* that in turn make you *feel* good. You are more than half-way to getting them. The outcome could be the perfection of a new technique or learning to skip. The important thing is to be honest about your abilities, and work with them. It is better therefore, to improve your favourite techniques, working on the more difficult ones as you gain confidence. Achievement in these short-term goals will give you confidence to work hard and consistently and stretch your imagination for your long-term goals.

Whilst striving to meet the challenge of the short-term goals you should also set medium- and long-term goals. In fact sometimes it is better to set the long-term goal first and work back to the short-term usually with a detailed schedule of medium-term goals. Short-term can be anything from a month to 3 months; medium-term 3 months to 12 months and long-term 1 year to 3 years. The important thing is to write it down, live it and stick to it!

It should be obvious then that your skill as a martial artist depends not only on coordination, speed, power and so on but also on your mental attitude whilst training. You must come to the realization that no real progress can be made until you understand the importance of integrating the mind and body.

A system of communication training known as NLP (Neuro-Linguistic Programming) will help you achieve not just your goals but the integration of mind and body. It has as one of its tools a technique that utilizes the power of the mind to enhance your physical performance by changing your behaviour. It involves mentally rehearsing each movement and effort involved in a specific technique or series of techniques. It develops the mental responses required for the precise control necessary in the performance of the technique. By continuous repetition in the mind, even the reflex response to a situation can be improved. The actual technique is covered in full under 'Resources'.

Feedback

This is the information we receive after performing an action. You will know that you have achieved what you set out to do because it will feel 'right' and you will feel good. That's about it really. If you don't feel good, do it differently. It's probably a signal from the unconscious to the conscious mind, so listen for it.

Rewards

The rewards of diligent and constructive training will be both physical and psychological. Increased awareness of the body and the environment, the development of self-confidence, esteem, a feeling of well-being and a positive attitude are all to be gained through training in this manner. In other words, you're going to feel good. You and others will detect these changes and this will spur you on to continue training and continue improving. Just think, if you feel great every time you train, you will learn very quickly.

Resources

The techniques and training methods in this book will help you achieve your best performance if followed consistently. Always evaluate the merits of a technique with regard to its efficacy in a combat situation. It is vital that you keep up to date with the latest training methods and equipment, for self-protection and competition. Read inspirational books, listen to inspirational music that will help you to develop an attitude of empowerment.

One very useful method that can be used, in your daily life, as well as in training, is a technique taken from the field of

NLP. It can be practised almost anywhere although initially it is best to practise in a quiet secluded area free from distractions.

Settle yourself into a comfortable posture, cross-legged or sitting in a chair is ideal. Be wary, however, of falling asleep. When you are comfortable lower the eyelids and observe your breathing, be aware of the rising and falling of the abdomen. It may be easier for you to count your breaths as they flow in and out. Breathe through the nose with the tongue resting on the palette.

After 5–10min of this practice you must attempt to visualize in your mind's eye the technique you wish to practise. Imagine seeing it like a film where you are the director. If you are directing the film you can determine the outcome. Imagine you are in a cinema. See what is about to happen or is happening and then change it until it is perfect. Use a role model and put yourself in their shoes. If you visualize the perfect technique, hear the sounds you would like to hear, you will start to induce the feelings that make you successful. Notice where they are and what they are doing. Remember them and bring them back when you need them most.

It is with this technique that you can help yourself to develop control under pressure. Develop fear control, and calm pre-fight nerves. Vividly imagined situations are regarded as real by your body and you therefore respond as if the situation is real.

The Ram Muay is the ideal time to practise this technique but should be taught by a qualified coach who understands the significance of the ritual and its practice.

After not less than 10min of visualization return to watching the breath and relaxing the body for about 5min. Finally stand up and perform some light joint rotations and stretching exercises.

In training, use these skills to enhance your solo training. When using the heavy bag or shadow boxing, visualize the technique before you do it. But remember, like any technique, constant practice is the key to success and mental rehearsal should play as important a part in your training schedule as the physical techniques.

Appendix 1

Basic Thai Customs

If you should visit Thailand. A few words of advice…

I have always had a strong belief in the traditional aspects of Muay Thai. Consequently, I respect the traditions of the culture that developed the art. I am interested not only in the sport of Muay Thai and the ancient fighting forms from which it evolved, but am also deeply involved in learning the language and in understanding the customs of Thailand. If you visit Thailand to train (which more and more people are now doing), I think it is vitally important that you go out armed with knowledge – knowledge of the customs and the language. I'm not saying you have to bury yourself in books avidly trying to learn the whole of the language. What you need to do, to earn a Thai's respect, is understand just a little of the language used for training purposes and a little of the etiquette of Thailand. Believe me, the Thai people will take you more seriously and pass on information to you that you would normally miss out on. In this section we're going to have a crash course in basic Thai customs and a glossary of words you will come across during training.

The Thai people are warm and friendly and always seem to be smiling. Don't take advantage of their hospitality by being ignorant of a few simple customs that you should respect.

Appearance: In Thailand you will be judged by what you look like. Most Thai spend a great deal of time and money on their appearance. You may get away with looking like a crumpled rag for the Thai are far too polite to say anything. You will, however, be refused entry to a temple if you are unacceptably dressed. If you are invited to a house, dress neatly and conservatively.

Monarchy: Highly revered by all in Thailand, the king is above criticism. As a *farang* (foreigner) you will be asking for trouble if you criticize him in any way. Indeed, it would be very rare for a Thai to discuss the monarchy with a foreigner.

Religion: 90 per cent of Thai are Buddhist and as any visitor to Thailand will tell you the country is carpeted with beautiful temples and Buddhist statues. Every house will have a shrine and at least one of the men in a household will have spent some time as a Buddhist monk. Respect this gentle religion and treat images of the Buddha, temples and the monks with respect. Shoes should be removed before entering a temple and you should *never* point the soles of your feet at a statue of the Buddha. Monks are strictly forbidden to have any physical contact with women so female visitors should take care not to sit next to one on a bus or accidentally bump into one!

Harmony: You will rarely see a Thai lose his/her cool. The preservation of surface harmony is all important. It is conceptualized in the philosophy of *jai yen* or cool-heart. Whatever happens *jai yen* prevails. If you meet an awkward situation with a cool heart you gain maximum respect. If you lose your temper, you lose respect. This is very important if you intend learning anything from a Thai.

Introductions and meetings: Always address the head of a house or an elder by the title *Khun*. If his name is Songchai then address him as *Khun* Songchai. Take your shoes off before entering a house and use the *Wai* bow that is customary between Thai. A whole chapter could be devoted to the concept and idea of the *Wai*. I have insufficient space here to do it justice; suffice to say that one should show respect to elders by performing a deeper *Wai* than you would to a man of, say, your own age. Thai will also say '*Bpai nai?*' (Where are you going?). This is a formality rather than a direct question and your reply should be '*Bpai tee-o*' (I'm going out) or '*Bpai tee-o mah*' (I've been out). The best known one is of course the '*Sawadee*' (How do you do? pleased to meet you) greetings. If you're a male it's *Sawadee Khrup* and a female *Sawadee Kha*.

Appendix 2

Grading Syllabuses and Club Rules of Phraya Pichai Muay Thai Camp International

GRADE 1 (WHITE)
Guard position

Footwork
Move: forward, backward, left, right, and changing stance

Hands
Jab: delivered stationary, moving forward, backward, left and right

Cross: delivered stationary, moving forward, backward, left and right

Combination: jab and cross combination, delivered stationary, moving forward, backward

Layback and parry: used when stationary, moving forward and backward

Elbows
Side elbow

Defence against side elbow

Knees
Straight knee: delivered with parry while grabbing the neck and moving forward and backward

Kicks
Round kick: low rear leg round kick delivered while stationary and moving forward

Defending against round kick: shin block

Front kick: lead leg (snap) to body

Defending against front kick: scoop block, left and right

Self-protection
Awareness: states (e.g. Cooper's colour codes), commentary walking

Use of the voice

Line-up/stance

Simple hand-techniques
- palm-heel strikes
- slaps with flat/cupped hands
- when to use fist/knuckles
- side of hand
- fingers/thumbs

GRADE 2 (YELLOW)
Guard position

Footwork
Yang Saam Khum: basic (3 strides movement)

Hands
Hook: left and right-hand hook stationary, delivered moving forward, backward, left and right

Combinations: jab, cross and hook combinations, stationary, moving forward, backward, left and right

Defending against hook: elbow block, swan-neck catch

Stepping punches: right and left

Elbows
Diagonal: cutting up and down

Rabbit elbows (circular)

Knees

Round knee: delivered while grabbing the neck and grabbing the body around the waist

Thrusting knee: delivered while grabbing the neck

3-level rabbit knee

Clinching Techniques

Basic inside position

Defence to basic position (shoulder lift)

Kicks

Round kick: middle level

Push kick: rear leg and front leg to body

Peck kick to legs (left and right) using ball of foot and instep

Defending middle level round kick using arm block

Defending against round kick using front kick to body and leg

Ram Muay

Basic understanding of Ram Muay – what it is and its purpose

Sparring (light contact)

1 × 2min round of technique sparring – hands only

Self-protection

Awareness: general personal security (out and about, home, in the car/travelling)

Use of elbows

GRADE 3 (GREEN)
Guard position

Footwork

Yang Saam Khum: includes
• rear leg shin block on forward movement
• front leg shin block on backwards movement

Hands

Uppercut: Front and rear hand, delivered stationary, moving forward, backwards, left and right

Combinations: jab, cross, hook and uppercut combinations

Defending against jab, cross, hook and uppercut:
• downward parry to arm (uppercut defence)
• cross arm block and counter with punch
• elbow block and counter with elbow
• swan-neck catch and counter with knee

Elbows

Spinning elbow from right cross

Knees

Long knee: delivered without grabbing, moving forward and backward

Defence against knees:
• push away
• hook-back knee

Clinching Techniques

Grabbing the neck: one hand push, one hand pull

Grabbing the neck: turning using two steps

Grabbing around the waist

Defence against waist-grab

Kicks

Roundkick: front leg attack, evade and counter-kick

Block roundkick and counter with round-kick off rear leg

Catch roundkick and counter (with kick, knee and throwing the leg)

Evade roundkick: step diagonally (to left and right) and counter

Defend against push kick with scoop and counter with kick

Ram Muay

Part 1: sealing the ring

Sparring (light contact)
1 × 2min round of technique sparring –
hands and kicks
1 × 2min round of technique clinchwork –
without knees

Self-protection
The OODA loop

Entries	Pre-emptive strikes
• pat, wrap, attack principle	• attack rituals
• step across/evasion	• personal space (4m)
	• intimate space (1m)

GRADE 4 (BLUE)
Guard position

Footwork
Yang Saam Khum: retreating

Hands
Feinting the jab

Punching Combinations: all to be per-
formed stationary, moving forward and
backward
• Feint jab and stepping in second jab
• Feint jab and straight rear-hand punch
• Feint jab and lead hand hook
• Feint jab and lead hand uppercut

Elbows
Jumping downward elbow
Defence against spinning elbow

Clinching techniques
Circle body grab (side-on)
Defend circle body grab
Defend double neck grab – using two
crossed arms
Defend double neck grab – using circle
grab body

Kicks
Rear leg low roundkick to ankle joint
Front leg low roundkick to inside of opponent's legs
Extended front kick off rear leg
Punching and Kicking Combinations:
• Jab and cross followed by a rear leg
  roundkick
• Block roundkick and counter with
  – front kick to body and to knee
  – with knee
  – with punch
• Front kick to standing leg and counter
  with rear leg roundkick to the body or
  punch

Ram Muay
Part 2: three bows

Padwork
Ad-lib padwork using the techniques
demonstrated in this grading and in previous grades (long pads and belly-shield)

Sparring (light contact)
1 × 2min round technique sparring – all
techniques
1 × 2min round technique clinchwork –
with knees

Self-Protection
The meaning of control (physical and psy-
chological)
Behavioural responses
Use of knees

GRADE 5 (BLUE/WHITE)
Guard position

Footwork
Yang Saam Khum: used to move in to
attack an opponent

Hands

Defend punch by evasion and countering immediately with knee

Defend against punch by evasion and using inside low kick to leg (kicking opponent off legs or off-balance)

Elbows

Flying side elbow

Knees

Knee to the leg to bring the body down followed by knee to the body

Clinching techniques

Moving in to grab opponent using punch

Defend double neck grab: catch neck and arm and throw as opponent knees

Kicks

Front leg roundkick: low and middle level

High roundkick to neck

Defend rear leg kick to body using right cross

Defend high kick by stepping and leg kick opponent

Defend against roundkick with front kick to opponent's kicking leg or body and counter (with rear leg roundkick to body or punch)

Front kick to chest

Hopping front kick

Ram Muay

Part 3: kneeling four directions

Padwork

3 × 2min ad-lib padwork using techniques demonstrated in this and previous grades

Sparring (light contact)

1 × 2min play-sparring (no shin-pads or gloves)

2 × 2min technique sparring to include clinchwork

Self-protection

Fear – what is it

When and when not to use kicks

Use of front kick/stamping

GRADE 6 (BROWN)
Guard position

Footwork

Introduction to skip-step with boxing techniques:
• skip-step jab, cross combination
• stealing the step (timing exercise)

Hands

General combinations using all techniques

Elbows

General combinations using all techniques

Knees

Jumping knee

Flying knee

Kicks

Defence against caught leg:
• turn and slip
• hook toes/elbow into clinch
• turn and knee, reach and clinch
Back kick (heel contact)

Front kick with toes

Front kick with heel

Side kick

Jumping front kick (left and right)

Peck kick to chin

Ram Muay

Part 4: standing 4 directions

Padwork

3 × 3min ad-lib padwork using techniques demonstrated in this and previous grades

Sparring (light contact)
1 × 2min play-sparring (no shin pads or gloves)
2 × 2min sparring to include clinchwork

Self-protection
Fear – dealing with it
Dealing with grabs

GRADE 7 (BROWN/WHITE)
Guard position

Footwork
Demonstrate understanding of *all* Yang Saam Khum
Skip-step with kicks and knees

Hands
Jumping punch

Kicks
Spinning heel kick

Combinations
2 defences and counters for each weapon (hands, elbows, legs, knees)

Ram Muay
Complete

Padwork
Freestyle padwork

Sparring
2 × 2min formal sparring

Self-protection
Decisiveness – why
Ruthlessness – why
Combinations of techniques
Use of environment and objects

GRADE 8 (BROWN/WHITE/YELLOW)
Guard position

Footwork
Kicks
Jumping roundhouse kick (left and right)
Flying front kick (left and right)

Combinations
Develop/improvise own combinations

Ram Muay
Complete plus intellectual understanding of the naming ceremony (Yok Kru)

Padwork
Freestyle padwork

Sparring
2 × 3min formal sparring
Introduction to sparring with elbows (head-guards to be worn)

Self-protection
Conditioning
Simplicity – why
Free-form defence
Stick defence:
• angles of attack
• defence against angles of attack

Grade 9 (Red/White)

Answer set questions to include the following topics:
• Ram Muay
• Yok Kru
• History of Phraya Pichai and Muay Thai
• Self-protection

Take warm-up to include:
• cardiovascular
• stretching
• specific Muay Thai fitness

Padwork
Freestyle padwork

Sparring
1 × 3min formal sparring to include elbows (head-guards to be worn)
Basic understanding of judging and refereeing
Critical analysis of sparring

Self-protection
Speed/Surprise/Aggression
Head controls
Basic defence from the floor
Knife defence:
• deal with threat
• deal with attack

GRADE 10 (RED)
Produce a paper of at least 1,500 words or a practical project on an aspect of Muay Thai/Self-protection.

Assist instructor in running a class

Combinations
Various of the examiner's choice

Self-protection
The Law as it relates to self-protection
Dealing with weapons

Instructor
Successful completion of one-day course

The one-day course comprises the following:
• How to build rapport
• How to produce the desired responses
• How to keep a class motivated
• Motivational techniques
• Building confidence
• Confident public speaking
Structuring a typical class for:
• Muay Thai
• Self-protection

This is NLP-based and the student will be asked to complete 8 out of 10 questions on a paper that will be marked one week after completion of the course.

Club Rules
1. Uniform must be kept in a clean condition and relevant armband *must* be worn
2. No jewellery to be worn during training sessions
3. Wai (bows) must be made:
   a. when entering and leaving the training area
   b. when joining the class
   c. to instructors
   d. to partners when training
4. No smoking is allowed
5. No consumption of alcohol before training
6. No swearing, bad manners or offensive behaviour
7. Students must ask permission to leave the training area
8. Derogatory remarks are not to be made against other martial arts and proper respect should be given to them
9. All students must conduct themselves in a sportsmanlike manner
10. Students must not misuse their knowledge of Muay Thai in contravention of law and order

Glossary of Muay Thai Terms

AM-NUAY PHAWN	Blessing	*KOW LOY*	Flying Knee
ANDAP	Ratings	*KOW LOD*	Low Knee
AO! JAI! SAI	'Pay attention!'	*KOW NOI*	Small Knee
BOOK!	'Attack!'	*KOW TONE*	Jumping Knee
CHA KWA NEE	'Slower!'	*KHLOOM!*	'Cover up!'
CHOHK!	'Fight!'	*KHLOOM! WAI!*	
CHORAKED FAAD	Turning Kick. lit.	*KHUEN KRU*	Ritual whereby
HAANG	Crocodile		teacher accepts
	thrashes tail!		student
DAIHOO-UH! JY!	Vital point just	*KRU*	Teacher
	under the heart	*KRUANG RUANG*	Armband
DON!-TREE MUAY	Music	*LOP*	To duck
	accompanying	*MAT*	Fist
	the fight	*MAT AT*	Uppercut
DUHN NA	Advance or move	*MAT DRONG*	Straight Punch
	forward!	*MONGKON*	Headband worn
DTAH	Eyes		during Ram
DTEE	Hit		Muay
DTEH!	Kick	*MUAY PLAM!*	wrestling
DTEH! KAO	Knee Kick	*NA KAENG*	Shin
DTEH! WIANG	Roundhouse	*NAK MUAY*	Thai boxer
	Kick	*NEB*	Pecking Kick
DTOI	Boxing		with the ball of
DTOI LOM	Shadow boxing		the foot
EEK THEE	'One more time'	*OON!*	Warm-up
FAI DAENG	Red corner	*PANG NGA*	Evade
FAI NAMNERNG	Blue corner	*PAOS*	Thai long pads
HOOK	The Hook as	*RAM MUAY*	Pre-fight Ritual
	used in boxing	*REH-O!*	'Faster!'
JANG! WA!	Timing and	*SAWK*	Elbow
	Rhythm	*SAWK CHIENG*	Variation of
KAHT! KWAHNG	To block		Sawk Tad
KAI MUAY	Boxing Camp	*SAWK HUD*	Rising elbow
KOW	Knee	*SAWK KLAB*	Reverse elbow
KOW DRONG	Front Knee	*SAWK KU*	Double elbows
KOW KONG	Overarm Knee	*SAWK SAB*	Chopping elbow

SAWK TAD	Cutting up elbow	*WONG MUAY*	Band that plays during the fight
SAWK TI	Cutting down elbow	*YAEB*	The Jab
SAWK TONG	Downward smashing elbow	*YANG SAAM KHUM*	Three strides movement. Footwork drill
T AE	Kick	*YUD*	Stop!
TAE PUB NOK	Kick to the outside of the knee		
TAE TAD	Low sweeping Kick		
TEEP	Push Kick		
TEEP DAN LANG	Back Kick		
TEEP DUEHSON	Push Kick with the heel		
TING	Throw		
WAI KRU	Showing respect to the teacher		

This glossary is not intended to show all of the variations in the Thai language and of course what it can't show are the variations in tones. If you wish to pursue your study of the Thai language there are many good books and tapes available. If all this does is show your Thai friends that you are making an attempt to understand the language it will earn you their respect and you will not be treated like every other Farang who wants to be a Thai boxer.

Bibliography

Andreas, Steve and Charles Faulkner (eds), *NLP The New Technology of Achievement* (Nicholas Brealey Publishing, 1994).

Bandler, Richard and John Grinder, *Frogs into Princes* (Real People Press, 1979).

Dilts, Robert, *Changing Belief Systems with NLP* (Meta Publications, 1990).

Kraitus, Panya, *Muay Thai: The Most Distinguished Art of Fighting* (Pimdee, 1988).

Zoran, Rebac, *Thai Boxing Dynamite* (Paul H. Compton, 1983).

Useful Web sites:
www. phrayapichai.com
www. mindworkstechnologies.com
www.welshthaiboxing.com
www.sassurvival.co.uk

For information on training as an instructor with the Phraya-Pichau Camp, contact the author on 07811 325158.

For the best training in Thailand:
www.wptgym.com

Index